Raising the Perfect
Canine Companion

Swimming is a completely natural activity relished by most dogs and humans.

Photo courtesy HSUS/Rummp

SUPERDOG

*Raising the Perfect
Canine Companion*

by

Dr. Michael W. Fox

**HOWELL
BOOK HOUSE**
New York

1990

Howell Book House
A Simon & Schuster Macmillan Company
1633 Broadway
New York, NY 10019

Library of Congress Cataloging-in-Publication Data
Fox, Michael., 1937-
       Superdog : raising the perfect canine companion / Michael W. Fox.
          p. cm.
       Includes index.
       ISBN 0-87605-743-1
       1. Dogs. 2. Dogs—Behavior. 3. Dogs—Training.
I. Title.
[SF426.F694—1996]
636.7'0887—dc20   96-13164
                              CIP

Manufactured in the United States of America

10 9 8 7 6 5 4 3

For Loppy and Friday

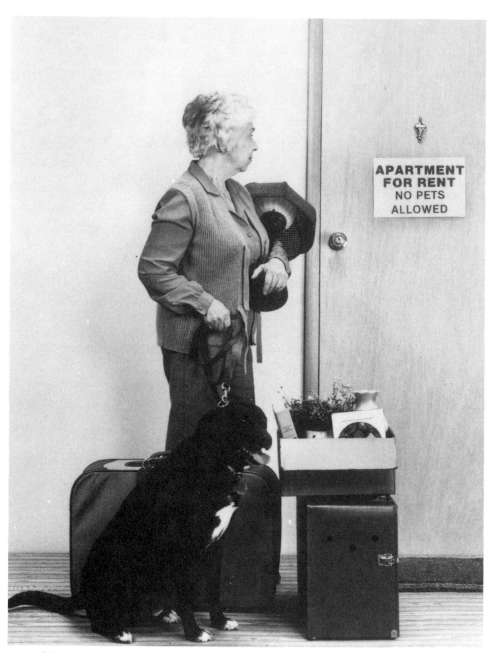

It is ironic that more of society's doors are closing to dogs and dog keeping at a time when we need dogs and the benefits they bring more than ever before.

Photo courtesy HSUS

Contents

Introduction   ix

Some Personal Reflections   xi

 1. Do Animals Think? Can They Reason?   1

 2. The Many Roles of Dogs   18

 3. Know How Your Dog Communicates   28

 4. How to "Decode" Dog Behavior   39

 5. Animals' Sounds Make Sense   47

 6. Understanding Your Dog's Super Sense—Smell   59

 7. Supernature and Psychic Abilities of Dogs and
    Other Friends   67

 8. Raising a Super Pet   79

 9. A More Natural Life for Your Dog   93

10. Training Your Dog   111

11. Developing a Watchdog   123

12. New Babies and Young Children: Nipping Problems
    Before They Start   129

13. The Four Rs of Dog Rights, Health and Owner
    Responsibility   136
14. For Better or Worse—How We Affect Our Dogs   152
15. Conclusions: Animal Awareness and Animal Rights   161
16. IQ Tests (Games and Exercises) for Dogs   171
17. Advanced IQ Tests and Exercises   190
    Appendix: Most Asked Questions About Dogs   201
    Index   209

Introduction

IT IS SOME FIFTEEN YEARS since my book *Understanding Your Dog* was first published, and over these years I have gained new insights and learned much from putting theory into practice, especially in terms of dog socialization and rearing practices. Dog owners, breeders and trainers have also contributed by sharing their experiences, insights and problems. But I am especially grateful to the dogs themselves, who, in many respects, are our mirrors and teachers as well as faithful companions and family members.

In this new book I have refined and clarified many of my own ideas and theories about canine behavior and development, combining my knowledge and experience as an animal behaviorist or ethologist and veterinarian for the benefit of one of my best friends and teachers, the dog, and for their human companions. (I prefer "companion" to the term "owner," since dogs are more than mere possessions or objects of property.)

Indeed, our canine companions are not mere insensitive instinct-programmed things, since, as I demonstrate at the beginning of this book, they are able to think, reason and have insight and imagination. An attitude of respect for and recognition of the inherent qualities of canine sapience and sentience—intelligence and feeling—is a prerequisite to a satisfying relationship with one's canine companion and to rearing a veritable *Superdog*.

Such a positive attitude is not the only prerequisite, however. Objective knowledge of canine behavior, of how dogs express their emotions and intentions, is essential to proper understanding and communication, which this book details. The sense of smell, which is so highly developed in the dog, and extra- or suprasensory "psychic" abilities of dogs and other animals are also explored.

Besides outlining the basic principles of sound breeding, rearing, temperament evaluation and training, I also describe how to make life more natural and fulfilling for your dog, and how best to integrate the dog into the family "pack," especially when new babies and young children are involved.

The essential rules of responsible dog care are discussed from the perspectives of overall physical and psychological well-being and animal rights philosophy. And for those who wish to go beyond teaching their dogs simple tricks, I have included several canine IQ tests that will be entertaining and rewarding for all involved.

With a better understanding and appreciation of dogs, our enjoyment of them will be even greater. And in turn, their life-experience under our dominion will be more enriched and fulfilling. To this end, this book is dedicated.

Some Personal Reflections

THE HISTORY OF THE DOMESTIC DOG reflects our own history and changing relationships with fellow creatures and the natural world. Once and even still a hunting ally and family guard, the dog has not been spared subjection to the exploitative and commercial processes of today's industrial world. The human species has exploded in numbers and harmfully impacted upon the natural world since the beginning of the Iron Age, the age of pyrotechnology. As we enter the present age with our powers over atom and gene, we may wonder about our own fate and the fate of the dog, our first if not last deep link with the natural world.

How I remember my childhood delight in England with a dog as a playmate exploring the meadows, ponds, cornfields, woodlands and moors. My dogs showed me so much: a pheasant's nest and a snake in the grass; a dead rabbit close by to a red fox's den. I had a dog that once caught a grouse on the moors, snatching the bird in midflight in his lightning jaws. I dressed, cooked and shared with him this little bird that the English aristocracy used to "bag" by thousands on private hunting preserves.

Some of my stray dogs were sick and needed veterinary care for lice, enteritis, poor nutrition, or the plague—distemper, for which there was no cure or protective vaccine at that time. And so I learned. One dog, his name was Rover, *had* to roam free, I suppose because he was allowed to do so as a pup before I found him lost and starving one winter's day. My parents could not bear keeping him confined because he suffered so when he couldn't be free. But he chased the neighboring farmer's milk cows and that cost the farmer money, he complained, because the cows gave less milk after Rover had chased them around the field. So Rover was put to sleep.

However, chasing the cows could have been good fun for the cows, whom little Rover could never hurt. A run around the meadows with a playful dog at their heels could well have been a tonic for these placid and often too flaccid and sickly dairy cows—their milk production quotas notwithstanding. Unlike sheep, who are terrified by dogs, cows will kick up their heels and cavort around bellowing and swinging their horns and even incite dogs to chase them. Rover would never have hurt them—only the farmer's ditches and barbed wire could have caused them injury.

The death of Rover brought with it the realization of how confining the lives of cows, dogs and all domesticated animals have become, for reasons of economy and convenience.

I remember being terrified one day chasing Rover all over the neighborhood until I could get a leash on him and put him in a dark and quiet place. He was completely petrified by something, his eyes were glazed, he didn't know me and he snapped and snarled and trembled all over as he ran and ran trying to escape from some invisible demons. Years later I learned that he was having "running fits," a form of canine hysteria caused by ageine, a bleach that was used to make bread white in England during World War II. Someone said that it looked like rabies and in an old book I found an engraving of an emaciated, terrified and snarling dog afflicted by this disease. I looked at that illustration for a long time, the feeling of concern for the poor dog overriding all fear.

Not long after that incident with Rover, I was walking home from grade school and on impulse, peered through the fence and into the back yard of the local veterinary clinic. What I saw became etched into my mind forever: a large trash can brimming over with dead cats and dogs with a halo of flies buzzing around them. I never knew the reason for this mass extermination but I was, from that time on, committed to doing all that I could to help animals, deciding at age nine that I had to be a veterinarian.

Looking back to my childhood with animals, after more than twenty-five years as a veterinarian, it is easy to see why I still care deeply for my fellow creatures. Much of my professional life has been devoted to helping to alleviate the suffering of animals through education and legislation to encourage greater respect and reverence for all life.

I have engaged in experimental behavior and brain development studies in dogs and puppies and I am no stranger to vivisection, or to the altruistic motives of many concerned and curious scientists. I am fortunate to have met some very great scientists and Nobel laureates, all of whom held Nature and all creatures in deep reverence. Yet they too had experimented upon animals, causing them harm for knowledge's sake. However, I now regard experimenting upon dogs and other creatures for the purported benefit of humankind as unethical, and as flawed by the notion that animal experiments and animal suffering and death are justified in our search for ways to alleviate human disease and suffering. Much of the suffering and disease we experience we bring upon ourselves—for example, by consuming too much alcohol and fatty meat and by living in an unsanitary and polluted environment. These are economic, social, political and ideological problems that no amount of animal research and suffering can rectify. We don't need to do chronic alcohol, tobacco-smoke-inhalation and high-fat-diet studies on dogs and other creatures to prove the obvious, or to test military weapons on Beagles, as has been done in the recent past. As for the claim that research on animals can help other animals, I would say yes, to some extent this is true. But we should not and need not make perfectly normal and healthy animals ill in order to find cures for many of the diseases we have in part created in domesticating animals, selectively breeding them and keeping them in the ways that we do, too often under conditions that deny them their basic behavioral and social requirements. This is especially true in many zoos, in large breeding facilities for dogs, and in many animal research laboratories and "factory" farms. Legislation in the United States, enacted in 1985, mandates that caged dogs in laboratories have some time every day outside enclosures often so small that they cannot make two full strides.

Many dog lovers and purebred dog clubs have helped support the Humane Society of the United States and other publicly supported animal protection organizations in the battle to obtain such minimal animal welfare standards and have also supported them in their war against illegal dog fighting; against government-licensed dog dealers and handlers who neglect the animals that they hold for sale to research laboratories; against unscrupulous and filthy "puppy mill" breeding factories and retail outlets; against companies that sell inferior and even harmful pet foods and veterinary pharmaceuticals . . . the laundry list is endless. These and other animal protection issues now occupy much of my time and effort as a vice-president of the Humane Society of the United States. I wish to thank dog lovers and those many others who care for fellow creatures for their continuing support. As Mahatma Gandhi once said, "The greatness of a nation and its moral progress can be judged by the way in which its animals are treated."

1

Do Animals Think?
Can They Reason?

DO ANIMALS REALLY THINK and show fore-
sight and insight? Can they be rational and can they reason? There
is a widespread belief that animals, with perhaps the exception of
chimpanzees, can do none of these things. Several scientific studies
of animals' behavior and learning abilities, and the experiences of pet
owners with their dog companions, dispel this belief. Yet many
people choose to hold on to this mistaken view of animals as unthink-
ing and even unfeeling machines. This attitude has its historical roots
in theology and philosophy, setting humans above animals so that we
can exploit them without a twinge of conscience.

Now it is true that much of an animal's behavior is instinctive,
mechanical, like a dog's wagging its tail or a cat's purring. Human
laughter, smiling and crying are no less instinctive. While these
actions are instinctual, when and to whom a dog wags its tail or bares
its teeth entails discrimination (as between a friend or foe). The
ability to discriminate involves the rudiments of intelligent reasoning, more so when the dog wags its tail in order to influence, even
manipulate, its owner for attention, for food, play or a walk outdoors. A dog will even bring a leash to ask its owner to take it out,
or a ball, presented as an invitation to play. Such behavior is more

There is a considerable body of demonstrable evidence that dogs do possess the ability to think even if the process is not the same as human reasoning power.

Photo courtesy HSUS/Stephanie Rodgers

than the result of simple, mechanical conditioning, since reasoning and insight underlie these complex symbolic actions where the animal has expectations and can anticipate the outcome of its actions. An animal that could not think, make associations and see into the future in terms of the causal sequence of events could not perform such actions in the first place.

However, dogs aren't always rational. Like us, they are often quite irrational and act without reason. A dog or human in a state of hysterical terror or paranoia cannot be reasoned with. As humans get carried away with their emotions and desires, so animals will sometimes get out of control: for example, a male dog will disobediently chew and tear and dig its way out of house and yard to reach a bitch in heat next door.

But let's not get too carried away: while animals are emotionally similar to us and have comparable if less developed mental abilities, it would be wrong, indeed irrationally anthropomorphic, to believe that animals have anywhere near our abilities to think abstractly and make intuitive associations.

While it takes highly sophisticated intelligence and technology for an aviator to plot a course from Alaska or Missouri to Peru or Mexico, migrant birds and monarch butterflies can do this instinctively. Their ability is inborn; ours is learned. They respond perhaps without objective awareness: their awareness is intuitive, no less remarkable than our acquired abilities and in essence, no less intelligent.

This leads us to another related issue: are animals really consciously aware? Once we learn to perform some action, such as driving a car, our repetition of the action becomes unconscious, which explains my difficulty in regaining conscious attention so as to not jam the gears on my wife's new car, whose stick-shift is patterned differently from those of my own car and her deceased one. So we aren't always consciously aware when we execute learned, habitual actions. Nor are animals that have learned some routine or are executing some complex instinctual behavior: we and they are creatures of habit.

Determining how consciously aware animals are is difficult, but the writings of two eminent scientific authorities, Professor Donald Griffin in his book *Animal Awareness* and Dr. Stephen Walker in *Animal Thought,* lead to the inevitable conclusion that animals are, to varying degrees, consciously aware and are capable of reason, insight and intelligent behavior. Clever creatures do think, and the more social and empathic and emotive they are, the more they can think.

Certainly computers are intelligent, and many animal species, especially insects, show a mechanical, computerlike intelligence. While there is certainly some awareness—electronic or neurological—scientists are still uncertain which animal species possess self-awareness. A fish or bird will attack or court its image in a mirror, such primary narcissism being suggestive of a lack of self-awareness. But as a bird will preen itself when dirty and a fish can discriminate when it is being touched and when it is touching something itself, the basic ingredients of self-awareness and thus reflective thought must be present in these animals. Puppies and kittens will react to a mirror as though it is another animal, but as they mature they will ignore their mirror image, which implies that they know it is not another animal but their own reflection. So they seem to be self-aware.

Many people have a very narrow view of animal intelligence, often based upon the restricted opportunities of their pets and other animals (in zoos, laboratories and "factory" farms) to show their natural talents. Little wonder that such people deny that these animals have the ability to reason, and that any learning of which their owners are aware is usually dismissed as simple conditioning.

Teaching pets "tricks" gives pet owners a sense of pride, accomplishment, control and amusement, but a wholly erroneous view of animals' abilities. Some dogs are not dependent enough to be motivated to learn often meaningless acts such as rolling over or extending a paw to shake hands. Food reward doesn't work for all pets either, and those that don't respond like the highly trained dogs that appear in movies and television may be unfairly judged to be stupid. Teaching an animal to do tricks for home entertainment or commercial purposes I find demeaning and exploitative. Even the most simple tricks such as barking for food, rolling over on command, or raising a paw to shake hands are based upon subordinating the animal. For instance, paw-raising and rolling over in dogs are part of the animals' natural submissive "body language" repertoire. Making animals perform such acts means making them display their submission, which, in gratifying the human ego, says much about our need to feel superior and in control. (However, I am not opposed to basic obedience training, which is useful in helping animals adapt to living with us, and vice versa.) The most extreme examples of animals being trained to perform unnatural acts are seen at circuses and some zoos, where lions and tigers jump through hoops of fire and bears balance on stools and rolling balls. Such spectacles, which are

4

A confined dog solves the problem of retrieving a food pan by pulling on a stick attached to the pan by a wire. This is an example of insightful behavior.
Photo courtesy HSUS

now banned in a few enlightened European countries, such as Denmark, are a sad reflection of our need to demonstrate our superiority over animals and will power to control and subordinate them. However, some of the tricks that can be taught to animals provide us with the opportunity to investigate their intellectual abilities of reason and insight.

There are a number of tests that will be described later in this book (see Chapters 16 and 17) that you can use to evaluate how well your pet can think and reason. For example, set up a barrier with sufficient space beneath for your pet to be able to extend its paw beyond the barrier. Place some meat in a pie tin and attach a string with a piece of wood tied to the end, placing the wood just within reach of the animal's extended paw. Most pets, if sufficiently hungry, will at once reach out and pull in the piece of wood to get the meat. This is termed insightful behavior. One bright dog pushed a kitchen stool toward the barrier so it could jump over, demonstrating insight and foresight. Insight and foresight and the ability to extrapolate are seen frequently when cats and dogs are playing, hiding and ambushing each other just as when they are hunting prey and anticipating the prey's actions.

The ability to think and reason entails being able to make logical associations, which a Sheltie recently demonstrated. Muffin went on a short plane ride, which must have been very unpleasant for her. Now, any time a plane flies over her home, she has an anxiety attack, barking and racing all over the place until the plane has gone.

Many canine companions demonstrate well-developed discrimination and anticipation, basic ingredients of thinking and reasoning, as when they become excited on hearing the sound of their owner's car. In their ability to discriminate different odors, as between identical twins, our pets are far more intelligent than we. Drug-detecting dogs are so insightful that they can recognize a change in the familiar range of smells behind a car dashboard and have located hidden money, pistols and other items that they haven't even been trained to detect.

Do animals sit and wonder or worry about things as we do? That is difficult to know, since they can't speak, but it's quite clear when a dog is anxious or apprehensive. All dogs also dream, twitching, yelping, barking and making running movements in their sleep; some dogs even have wet dreams. Clearly they must be able to imagine things, another basic component of the ability to think, and to recall, and to recognize. There is another belief promulgated by some eminent scientists that, since animals have no language, no word-symbols, they cannot think. But this is clearly erroneous: there is a whole realm of preverbal memory and mental activity that animals share with us, and that our verbal abilities can either repress or enhance, as most psychoanalysts and therapists will attest.

The following well-documented examples from my records will help demonstrate animals' abilities to think, at times very logically, and to use foresight (i.e., to set goals) and hindsight (i.e., to learn from experience) in their carefully thought out behavior.

1. *Behavioral control and manipulation (of owner).* Many dogs bark or solicit incessantly until they are picked up and petted; some even feign injury to a limb to solicit their owners' attention (sympathy lameness).

2. *Observational learning.* Many dogs have taught themselves, after observing their owners, to press doorbells, open doors, flush toilets and operate drinking fountains. I have no records of tool use per se (which is a clear demonstration of forethought) in dogs and cats, although sea otters will use stones to crack open abalone shells, and even "small-brained" herons drop a feather in the water as a lure to catch fish. Some forms of intelligent behavior go beyond simple observational learning and mimicry. In one documented instance, a Collie uses one paw to pull the refrigerator door handle so he can "show" his owner food when he's hungry, which he does by opening the refrigerator door and barking. The owner knows when to feed the dog, because the dog tells her very clearly. Perhaps the dog has trained the owner.

3. *Symbolic behavior.* Many dogs express their wants and intentions with some nonverbal symbol rather than relying exclusively on body movement or vocalizations; for example, by presenting their owners with a ball or other toy when they want to play.

4. *Mimetic behavior (awareness of self and other).* Some dogs are able to copy a human communication gesture not present or used in their normal repertoire; for example, the dog's mimic expression of the human grin given when greeting their human companions. Paw-raising to "shake hands" may be another example of mimetic behavior.

5. *Emotional disturbance.* Symptoms are often comparable to those seen in humans, including separation anxiety, grief, depression, anorexia nervosa, fear, jealousy, guilt and psy-

chosomatic disorders such as diarrhea, pruritus, epilepsy and hysterical paralysis. All indicate subjective states of mental activity in many ways comparable to our own.*

6. *Insightful behavior (and reasoning).* A wild dog waits behind a rock to ambush prey being driven toward it by packmates. A dog pushes a stool next to a low gate so that it may get from the kitchen into the living room. A friend relates how she deliberately moved a stool away from the kitchen counter where she had just prepared a batch of French pastries, just in case the dog might get at her culinary creations. She returned later to find the stool by the counter, most of the pastries eaten and her dog hiding under the dining-room table. A researcher has detailed how several experimental rats, mice and hamsters, alone in glass jars into which tobacco smoke was being pumped in a smoke-inhalation study, crammed their own feces into the tube that delivered the smoke into the jar. This is insightful, "tool-using" behavior.

7. *Moral sense of reciprocity—fair exchange.* A dog steals a toy airplane from bed of sleeping boy; mother sees dog take airplane into kitchen, hide it and carry back dog's chew toy, which dog places on child's bed. Another dog solicits cheese from coffee table and is told "No!" Dog goes to kitchen, returns with dog biscuit, places it on owner's lap and looks at cheese. While the behavior of a captive family of wolves was being observed, one cub killed and began to eat a small rodent. Its growls kept the mother and littermates away. The mother dug up a piece of meat she had cached in one corner of the enclosure and carried it over to the cub, using it to entice the cub away from its prize. She gave the meat to the cub and quickly ate the rodent herself. She could have used sheer force to get the prey away from the two-month-old cub. Instead she used insight and coercion, thus avoiding any aggressive confrontation.

8. *Imagination.* Evidence of imagination (or what ethologists term a mental "search image") can be inferred from the behavior of a dog called to search and find some object

*For details, see M. W. Fox (editor), *Abnormal Behavior in Animals* (Philadelphia: W. B. Saunders, 1968). Also *Understanding Your Cat* and *Understanding Your Dog* (New York: Bantam Books, 1974 and 1974).

Separation anxiety is one form of emotional disturbance displayed by both people and dogs. Fear, guilt and jealousy are other emotional symptoms dogs and people commonly share. *Photo courtesy HSUS/Richard Lakin*

(such as a rat or marijuana stash). Likewise a puppy at play may pounce upon and chase nonexistent "prey." Such vacuum activity or hallucinatory play indicates imaginative ability.

9. *Sense of humor.* Seemingly aggressive behavior that occurs in playful teasing and mock attack necessitates a degree of awareness that such behavior is not serious, otherwise an aggressive or defensive response will be elicited. The cognitive shift in correctly interpreting such behavior as nonserious implies a sense of humor, an intrinsic feature of social play in cats, dogs and other mammals.

10. *"Minding" behavior.* A change in an animal's emotional state and behavior may be induced when the owner employs the dog's own body language (for example, by mimicking the play-soliciting bow) or uses human communication signals that the dog understands (such as a direct stare or growl-threat) to express an emotional state or intention. This is not simply conditioning, but rather, reflects the dog's ability to engage in trans-species communication, which would not be possible if the dog were unable to "read the mind" of its human interactee. The dog is able to infer, from the latter's overt behavior, human intentions and emotions. Empathy fits into this category. Empathic behavior is surely one of the most advanced forms of intelligent interaction, implying awareness of another's needs and emotional state. A blind pelican lived for years on an island and was fed daily by its flockmates. In England, a German Shepherd became a guide for its Cocker Spaniel companion when it went blind, opening doors for it and holding it by one ear to cross the road. In the United States, a crow became the close companion of a blind dog, even feeding and preening the animal. Such altruism in animals is surely a sign of a highly developed ability to "tune in to" and understand others, an aspect of intelligence and emotional awareness that is not exclusively human.

11. *Evidence for a sense of self?* Animals have a memory, and thus a reference point to self (an observing ego?) in time. They manifest territoriality, and thus a sense of self in space. In their sociability and social hierarchies (of pack or family), they must also have a sense of self in relation to others more dominant or subordinate.

Another striking similarity between humans and

Sticks are creative play "tools" for dogs, being used together in parallel play, or singly to catalyze a tug of war and chasing games.

Photo courtesy HSUS

many animal species is the ability to communicate and cooperate by literally bringing minds together, as exemplified by the complex societies of hive-bees and "city"-dwelling termites, and the wolfpack hunting together. Complex animal societies, like human societies, reveal how separate wills and consciousnesses become integrated to serve the collective good.

WORD COMPREHENSION

My dog Benji learned to understand several words and sentences.

I can say to him "Where's your bone?" and he will run into the bushes to look for it. I can say "Let's go to the park" and he will run to the gate. Clearly he knows what I am saying: he can translate my words as I can translate his language because both our vocabularies have the same elements of context, intentionality and expectation. When we are in the park and I say "Let's go to the park," he looks at me, then ignores me, obviously aware that what I have said is redundant because we are in the park, so there can be no expectation about going to the park.

Likewise, when he has his bone and I say "Get your bone," he either ignores me or growls, which could mean "Bug off," or that he thinks I'm trying to trick him and get his bone away from him. I have seen our other dog Tiny do this by suddenly getting up, looking toward the fence and growling as though there were a dog passing by. Benji will immediately leave his bone to investigate and Tiny then has the chance to steal his bone.

As we can use language to deceive each other, so can animals. But can they use language to project or imagine themselves in another context or place?

I can say "Go outside" to Benji or "Go away" and he will. Other dogs will go upstairs or downstairs when told to, in order to find a ball or slipper, for example. And if there are two balls or slippers they will bring one and will "fetch the other" when told to. But I am not aware of many examples of animals being able to communicate to each other in these ways. The best example is of the specific monkey calls, analogous to going upstairs or downstairs, given earlier.

How wolves communicate when they hunt, as when some drive prey toward others waiting in ambush, has not yet been determined.

Aggressive circling, maintaining direct eye contact, and ears and tail in an erect position are typical confrontational behaviors between mature male dogs such as these Telomians. These behaviors are often a prelude to . . .

. . . aggressive interaction between the dogs. This is usually a ritualized display, and actual physical injury does not generally occur.
Photos courtesy HSUS

13

A dog trainer can signal with hand and eye alone to make a dog stay or run one way or another and then stay or come, and I have seen dogs do the same thing with each other by eye contact, staring and pointing in a particular direction with their heads and direction of gaze. By these signals alone, a wolf orchestrating the hunt could easily signal others to stay, to follow or to run off in a particular direction. I remember once in the park, Tiny pointed at a small dog. Benji saw her signal and ran in the direction she was pointing, but slightly off course. His eyesight isn't too good and it was with sudden surprise that he almost ran past the little dog. By observing each other's signals constantly, animals stay in touch, an essential "attention-structure" among pack hunters like dogs and wolves, and in prey species such as deer and caribou. Through this "one-minded" attention they can be alert to danger instantly.

We see exactly this attention-structure between dog and master. Some owners, especially of highly attentive breeds like German Shepherds, Shelties, and Border Collies (which have been especially bred to have what is called "eye"), feel their dogs almost have ESP because they are so tuned in to what their human companions are doing and saying. Our pets often understand what we are saying. They are able to comprehend certain words that evoke learned actions and can set up expectations (like saying "walkies" to one's dog).

One of the earliest attempts to establish symbolic communication was by Sir John Lubbock (Lord Avesbury) in 1885, with his Poodle, Van. He endeavored, with some success, to teach his dog to read. His report, presented to the British Association for the Advancement of Science, included the following observations:

> I have tried this in a small way with a black poodle called Van, by taking two pieces of cardboard, about ten inches by three, and printing on one of them in large letters the word "food," leaving the other blank. I then placed two cards over two saucers, and in the one under the "food" card I put a little bread and milk, which Van, after having his attention called to the card, was allowed to eat. This was repeated until, in about ten days, he began to distinguish between the two cards. I then put them on the floor, and made him bring them to me, which he did readily enough. When he brought the plain card I simply threw it back, while when he brought the "food" card I gave him a piece of bread, and in about a month he had pretty well learned to realize the difference. I then had some other cards printed with the words "out," "tea," "bone," "water," and a certain number also with words to which I did not intend him to attach any significance such as "naught," "plain," "ball," etc. He soon learnt that bringing a card

Wolves engaging in a greeting ritual focused on their pack leader—a reflection of the species' intense sociability. *Photo courtesy HSUS*

Indian pariah dogs engaging in reciprocal sniffing. *Photo courtesy HSUS*

15

was a request, and to distinguish between the plain and printed cards; it took him longer to realise the difference between words, but he gradually got to recognise several. If he were asked whether he would like to go out, he would joyfully pick up the "out" card, choosing it from several others, and would bring it to me, or run with it in evident triumph to the door. The cards were not always put in the same places, but were varied indiscriminately, and in a great variety of positions. Nor could the dog recognise them by scent, for they were all alike, and continually handled by us. Still I did not trust to that alone, but had a number printed for each word. When, for instance, he brought a card with "food" on it, we did not put down the identical card, but another bearing the same word: when he had brought that, a third, then a fourth, and so on. For a single meal, therefore, eighteen or twenty cards would be used, so that he evidently was not guided by scent. No one who has seen him look down a row of cards and pick up the one he wanted, could, I think, doubt that in bringing a card he feels he is making a request, and that he can not only distinguish one card from another, but also associate the word and the object. This is, of course, only a beginning, but it is, I venture to think, suggestive, and might be carried further, though the limited wants and aspirations of the animal constitute a great difficulty. (*Report of the British Association for the Advancement of Science,* 1885, p. 1089; see also *The Life-Work of Lord Avebury* [Watts, London, 1924].)

Charles Darwin, in the *Descent of Man,* concluded: "We have seen that the senses and intuitions, the various emotions and faculties, such as love, memory, attention, curiosity, imitation, reason, etc., of which man boasts may be found in an incipient, and, even sometimes in a well-developed condition in the lower [sic] animals." But do they have a conscience?

MORALITY AND CONSCIENCE

Having a moral sense of right and wrong, a conscience, is certainly one criterion for the possession of soul, if not an actual index of spiritual development/evolution. Animals are generally, in this respect, not unlike very young children—extremely narcissistic or self-centered. But in some species, as they mature, particularly in highly social species such as wolves and dogs, the rudiments of morality and of social conscience are manifested. Many people can tell by the submissive and anxious behavior of their dogs that their animals have done something wrong (knocked over a lampshade, upset the kitchen trash container or stolen some food). These reactions are more than simple conditioning: the animal anticipates some form of retribution, which can be interpreted as guilt, the most rudimentary form of conscience. This reflects some awareness of what is socially acceptable or unacceptable, right or wrong. A more powerful dog's recognition of another's territory or another's bone shows social conscience, in which others' interests or rights are respected. The "policing" function of the alpha or pack-leader wolf who intervenes to stop two lower-ranking packmates from fighting or pins the aggressor to the ground can be interpreted as a display of moral conscience and social justice. In sum, it would seem that the more sapient, sentient and socially dependent a species is, the more it is likely to manifest conscience: conscious awareness of others' interests and an ability to discriminate what is morally and socially right and wrong. This ability is linked with the capacities of empathy and altruism.

If an animal can know what might harm another, and can anticipate the consequences of its actions, then it can constrain its own actions in order to avoid harming another or direct appropriate actions to help another (good dogs don't bite). Moral sense and sensibility and altruism are thus closely linked.

That animals like wolves and dogs do have a conscience or moral sense of right and wrong is thus further supported by many recorded acts of altruism: dogs have rescued people from burning houses and children from holes in the ice; wolves in a pack in Alaska brought food to their injured leader each day until he was well enough to hunt with them again.

2

The Many Roles
of Dogs

ARCHAEOLOGICAL evidence points to the dog as the first animal to be domesticated. Skeletal remains of dogs found around Middle Stone Age settlements are more dingolike than wolflike. No transitional wolf-dog form has ever been found, even though there is a scientific consensus that *Canis lupus pallipes,* the Asiatic wolf, is the dog's main ancestor. I feel that the dog's main ancestor was a wild dog not unlike the Australian dingo and Asiatic and New World pariah dog. These were hybridized with wolves, and even jackals and coyotes, at various times and places. It is ironic that as there is no original "wild dog" in the natural world, so there are no original wild horses or cattle. Those that do exist in the wild are actually domesticated forms that have become feral—that is, returned to the wild. Cattle, sheep, goats and horses—and the cat— were domesticated several thousand years after the dog first slept by our fires and played with our children.

The dog was our animal companion during that long period of early civilization that historians and mythologists call the Golden Age. We were then gatherer-hunters, living in small extended families and bioregional clans. And the dog lived and traveled with us not merely as a scavenging camp follower but also as an invaluable

One of the dog's oldest activities on behalf of humans was to control and move herds of sheep and other livestock. To assure the physical safety of the herds, the dog's natural predatory instincts were inhibited as the needs of man dictated. *Photo courtesy HSUS*

protector, alerting us with keen senses to the presence of dangerous predators like the lion and sabre-tooth tiger. With its speed and tracking ability, the dog was an ally in the hunt, and it kept us warm at night with its higher body temperature and was protector and playmate for our children.

When the Golden Age came to an end and we began to domesticate other species, the dog became the guardian and coherder of sheep, cattle and goats. Pups were chosen and selectively bred for those physical and psychological attributes most appropriate for these tasks, and new regional breeds evolved. The domain of the hunter shrank when wildlife and wildlands were taken over by the ever-expanding livestock industry. Hunting breeds, like the "gaze hounds"—the Saluki, Scottish Deerhound, Greyhound and Whippet, and later retrievers and pointers—were developed and prized by the aristocracy who maintained private hunting preserves in their dominions. The more human society began to diversify when the Neolithic agrarian "Silver Age" gave way to urban centers and empires of industry and commerce, so the varieties of domesticated dog began to diversify. Careful selective breeding formed the basis for the various breeds and classes of dogs that we enjoy today: toy and miniature breeds as pure companions especially for royalty and the wealthy; dogs of war, of flock, herd and hunt; dogs of hearth, homestead, turnspit, cart and sled. Some were even bred to fight or to be used for food.

Different cultural attitudes toward dogs make for differences in relationships. In some restaurants they serve chicken, beef and dog; and in others they serve chicken and beef to dogs, or at least let their human companions feed them from their tables. A European lady on vacation fainted after her dog was brought to her table, cooked by mistake, rather than having been taken into the back kitchen of a Hong Kong restaurant to be fed.

While some see the dog as meat, others see it as a loving companion, worthy of equal and fair consideration. To eat one's dog, or any dog, is the equivalent of cannibalism in many societies.

As some quasi-cannibals raise dogs to be roasted and eaten, other people, in the name of science and medical and military necessity, roast, gas, poison, irradiate, shoot, electrocute and crush dogs by the thousands in laboratories throughout the industrial world every month. Yet, ironically, in the industrial world dogs are highly valued as emotionally supportive and facilitating cotherapists for emotionally disturbed, handicapped and institutionalized people. To those whom they help, and for many who enjoy their company

To develop more useful companions in the hunt, the natural behavior of some dogs was modified. This resulted in the development of pointing dogs (above) and others with the innate ability to retrieve (below). *Photos courtesy HSUS*

simply as home companions, playmates, watchdogs and protectors, the practice of experimental vivisection of dogs is morally repugnant, an affront to their sensibilities. More and more people are beginning to question the ethics and scientific validity of making dogs and other creatures sicken and suffer to test cosmetics, household chemicals, weed killer and military weapons, and to find cures for the many diseases that we bring upon ourselves.

Many animal protectionists are vegetarians and have made their dogs vegetarians. While cats don't fare well on a meatless diet, many dogs thrive.

Dogs now assume many roles, some new and others old. There are vegetarian dogs, seeing-eye and hearing-ear dogs, canine cotherapists and bomb-locating and drug-sniffing dogs. There are kennels of hemophiliac and epileptic dogs, selectively bred to have these inherited diseases in order to serve as medical models for analogous human diseases. Then there are kennels where dogs are allowed out occasionally to hunt foxes, with the horses and their riders in pinks, or to help their masters kill bear, cougar, wild boar, raccoon and other wild creatures some people call game. Many of these dogs wear electronic collars their handlers control, and under such hi-tech control are zapped with electrical shocks if they don't hunt well or perform correctly in field trial training and competition.

Other more fortunate kennel dogs are let out more frequently to engage in dogsled team racing, but some never ever leave their kennels. These are the breeding stock, the "stud dogs" and "brood bitches" of the dog breeding farms that produce popular yuppie puppies and cross-bred fluffies like Cock-A-Poos and Shi-Poos for live-animal retail stores. Better pet stores work with local breeders and help clients choose and locate a puppy within the community. While home-bred puppies and vets who make house calls are becoming more popular, so is the "natural dog" or mixed-breed pup, a ready supply of which can be found at most urban animal shelters.

As cultural perceptions and treatment of dogs change and diversify, so we find new things emerging. We find dogs being used by foresters to find gypsy moths and other parasites and by farmers, not just to herd sheep and keep coyotes and feral dogs away, but also to detect when cows are in heat. And we find dog psychologists and animal behavior consultants for people with problem pooches and licensed counselors to help people cope with the grief of losing their doggy companions.

Nearly three decades ago, when I was a veterinary student, my peers scoffed at predictions of such developments and dismissed them when they did occur as sentimental excesses of an affluent society. But I see such developments as involving an increasing recognition that dogs, like other animals, do have feelings and can have emotional hangups just as we humans can, and that to love a dog as a significant other and to need help with coping with the grief, guilt, helplessness and anger normally associated with the loss of a beloved companion are not abnormal responses. To love is not sick. To love an animal is not some misguided emotional displacement and to grieve at its demise is not sentimentalism.

In these in some ways more sensitive times, one traditional role that dogs have had to fill for centuries is being outlawed and eradicated. This is the role of the fighting dog, bred and trained to tear other dogs apart for public enjoyment and private profit. Other more acceptable traditional roles persist, sometimes in modified form. Many people, for example, have sheepdogs—Border Collies, Kelpies and such, but have no sheep for the dogs to work, and thus no way of knowing if they are preserving the sheep-herding abilities of the dogs that they breed and raise. So they form clubs and learn how to work their dogs with sheep and even have sheep-herding trials for their urban and suburban dogs. Others enjoy working with their dogs through basic obedience school and then go on to competitive "meets," their dogs graduating to varying degrees of proficiency in retrieving, tracking, physical agility and simple problem solving. Highly proficient dogs are used in rescue work, helping locate people lost in wilderness areas and buried in the rubble of earthquake-devastated towns and cities.

It is difficult to imagine life without dogs: they continue to contribute in many ways to enrich our lives with their many skills and attributes. The various roles that they assume for us have certainly changed since they were first domesticated many thousands of years ago. From campsite guards and scavengers, hunting and herding allies to playmates for children, beasts of burden and dogs of war, they have shared and helped shape human history for millennia. They will continue to be an integral part of our lives and culture, and no matter how domesticated and dependent they may be, they will continue to be a vital and authentic link between us and the rest of the animal kingdom, evoking respect and reverence for all creatures wild and tame.

Behavioral studies of wolfpacks in the wild reveal a complex social order based upon dominance, affection, cooperation, allegiance to pack and leader and cooperative care of offspring. While I do not believe that the wolf is the sole ancestor of the domesticated

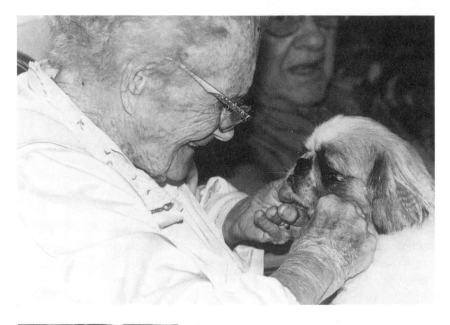

In recent years we have learned a great deal about the beneficial and therapeutic effects dogs have on the aged, the emotionally disturbed, autistic children, the terminally ill and others. As we gain greater understanding of this amazing potential, we will probably be able to make many significant breakthroughs in reaching hitherto unreachable people.

Photos courtesy HSUS: Top, Humane Society of Wichita County, Texas; bottom, Milwaukee Sentinel

24

dog, comparative studies of wolves and dogs and of free-roaming Asiatic pariah dogs and feral dogs (domesticated dogs that have gone wild) reveal that the psyche and social life of the dog are very similar to those of the sociable wolf. These similarities account for the dog's easy adaptation to living in a "surrogate" human family pack. Furthermore, since the average dog that is not physically encumbered by inherited anomalies of size, coat and conformation is fully capable of becoming feral, we can surmise that the psyche or spirit of the dog is not in any significant way degenerate or inferior to that of its wild canid cousin the wolf. Fully able to scavenge and hunt for itself or cooperatively in a pack, the feral dog bears witness that in most dogs the natural spirit and instinctual wisdom of millions of years of evolution cannot be snuffed out by a few thousand years of domestication.

But these qualities can be harmed by improper breeding and rearing, and as this book reveals, there are many ways to bring out the best of nature's potential in every dog, no matter what breed or how small or large it is. In outlining ways to produce a "Superdog" I would never make the arrogant assumption that we can and must improve upon nature. We should understand, respect and obey nature before we endeavor to make any "improvements," since our human-centered views of progress and perfection have, as history shows, caused more harm than good to our fellow creatures and to the natural world.

Having learned about the ways of wolves, many people now keep wolves as pets, while others breed and keep wolf-dog hybrids as the best alternative to actually keeping wolves, since more and more states now outlaw the keeping of any wild animal as a pet. Those who love wolves might do better to fight for their protection and habitat preservation in the wild rather than breeding and hybridizing them for sale as pets. Many first-generation wolf-dog hybrids are emotionally unstable, and like wolves, they do not always thrive in a domestic environment. Trying to introduce wolf qualities into the domesticated dog will inevitably result in some hybrids that are "wild"—hyperactive and frustrated when confined, very shy of strangers and difficult for inexperienced people to handle. I believe it is better to find less potentially harmful ways of improving the psyche of the dog than by introducing the traits of a wild animal into a fully domesticated one.

While the perpetual puppy "Peter Pan" pooches that never seem to grow up evoke the scorn of the purist who mourns the demise of wolves and wilderness made over into our own image, dogs will

All the tasks dogs perform for humans today are based on natural canine behavior patterns. The Foxhound pack (above) functions very much like any pack of feral canids would, while the Border Collie (below) exhibits modified hunting behavior when approaching sheep. *Photos courtesy HSUS*

always be dogs. The spirited nature of the dog will be lost only when the human spirit loses its own sense of wonder, respect and reverence for the natural world. The dog, like all natural things, is "ours" only in sacred trust. And even if we see the dog as an object of property, a valuable status symbol, a coworker, playmate or companion, that sacred trust is inviolable. Every dog, save some that have been severely abused, lives up to that trust, embodying those higher qualities so often lacking in our own kind: respect, loyalty, obedience, forgiveness, humility, empathy and unconditional love. We break that sacred trust more often than they. Perhaps, in the final analysis, dogs are closer to divinity than we. And while we may claim to have been made in God's image, we fall short of that image when we are insensitive and indifferent to the divine aspect of fellow creatures. In sum, the dog embodies those noble qualities that in part make us human, suffers from our inhumanity, and by virtue of its very existence manifests an aspect of divine presence. Each dog is God's gift and blessing, which we should all appreciate and celebrate. But when we forget these things and selfishly, even cruelly exploit dogs and other creatures without conscience and compassion, we make the sacred profane, and are lower than the lowliest of Earth's creation.

3

Know How Your Dog Communicates

W HEN YOU KNOW how your dog talks, you will not only find it easier to understand what your dog wants or feels, but also be able to control your dog more easily and have a deeper, more satisfying relationship. Dogs have a very rich repertoire of body language signals that are called displays. From the aroused or alert posture with erect tail and ears, the dog can move into various positions that display emotional reactions and behavioral intentions. Contrast the stiffly wagged tail, direct stare and snarl of an aggressive dog to a posture in which the body weight shifts backward and the tail is lowered: this is a fearful or defensive aggressive rather than an offensive aggressive posture. From this position the animal could go into the display of complete submission, curling up with ears flattened against its head and remaining completely still or "cowed" on the ground. Then some dogs will roll over into another passive submissive posture and urinate submissively, very much like a young puppy. Other body language displays in the dog include active as distinct from passive submission, in which the dog crouches but moves its tail in a submissive tail-wagging greeting. Then there is the

Prior to assuming a passive/submissive posture, the subordinate dog raises one forepaw, displays a submissive grin and holds ears back. The dominant dog shows a sideways display along with apprehensive nose-licking.

Photos courtesy HSUS

Displays of dominant and submissive postures during an aggressive encounter. The dominant dog shows a vertically-carried tail and raised hackles, while the submissive dog growls defensively and holds its ears back in a passive posture.

familiar display of play soliciting where the dog bows, wags its tail and may raise one front paw in a solicitous gesture.

One theory about the origin of the play bow is that it is derived from a stretching action in which one animal yawns and communicates its relaxed behavior to another. This can serve as a signal to establish a relaxed mood so that what follows stretching is not seen as serious. In other words, a play bow signals that what comes next, such as a seemingly aggressive snap or lunge, is not really serious but is playful.

The active submissive display or bow of greeting and play solicitation is a much more open body gesture than the passive submissive display of rolling over onto one side, and is one of the body language postures that people can mimic in communicating with their dog. I like to encourage children to mimic the dog's play bow when signaling their intention to play with their own dog or a dog that they know.

Look closely at your dog's displays or body language postures and you will note that the dog can alter its mood, and as it does so it either expands or contracts. The expansive outgoing displays are either assertive, aggressive, confident or playful. The more contracted displays are related to fear, aggression and passive submission. Some dogs, rather like people, will assume as part of their character either a contracted or an expanded demeanor, so it is possible to evaluate with some accuracy the personality of an individual dog by the way in which it generally carries its body, head and tail. Some dogs are naturally submissive and embarrass their owners, who feel that their cowering dog is a sign that will make other people think that they mistreat their pets!

The passive submissive behavior of rolling over on one side is a friendly gesture. A friendly or submissive dog will present its posterior groin or inguinal region to a more dominant dog. It rolls over onto one side and elevates the uppermost hind leg. This display, especially in young dogs, is often accompanied by submissive urination. Owners frequently make the mistake of disciplining their dogs for this behavior, and they should not, because such piddling is a sign of deference to the owner.

Konrad Lorenz in his book *Man Meets Dog* suggested that the subordinate dog presents its throat, the most vulnerable part of its body, to the dominant animal as a sign of complete surrender. This is not true, however. What the wolf or dog does is to present the groin region as a sign of submission. This behavior is related to parental care, and here we have the secret of this groin display revealed: the display of passive submission associated with urination is derived from mother-infant interaction in the following way. With a very young puppy that is unable to urinate for itself, the mother will approach its groin area and will lick the genitals and reflexively stimulate urination. This highly adaptive form of behavior helps keep the den clean, for the puppies only eliminate when they are stimulated by the mother who ingests everything. As the puppy matures and is able to eliminate independent of stimulation by the mother, it will still remain passive when touched in the groin region. And it may actually urinate, but now as a submissive signal.

When a dog approaches you in a friendly fashion, it will orient its hips toward you and will present its flank or groin. Touching the groin is the equivalent of a human handshake. It's a friendly thing to do. One should, however, avoid handling a strange dog in the groin area if it does not present the groin to you. The groin area is the first psychologically important area of communicating through body language with the dog. There are other key areas, such as the muzzle, and I will talk about these shortly.

In aggressive encounters, one dog may mount another as though it were sexually aroused. Mounting and clasping in this way is often misinterpreted as sexual behavior but in fact sexlike mounting and clasping actions are often a sign of dominance in dogs, primates and other animals. People also often misinterpret tail wagging as always being a friendly gesture. A stiff tail wag can mean dominant and aggressive intent.

When a dog is leashed and is out walking with the owner, it may be more aggressive toward other dogs because the owner is part of its territory. Owners who do have their dog on the leash should be advised, when they are approached by a strange dog, to remain quiet and to realize that if they start shouting and pulling their dog on the leash they could incite their dog to attack. When two dogs meet, generally one will remain passive and will allow the other to investigate it. Then the one doing the investigating becomes passive and allows the other one to sniff it. Such potentially peaceful interaction can be disrupted if one dog does not stand and allow the other one to sniff it, as when the owner starts to pull its dog away by the leash.

When a person is approached by a strange dog, it is helpful in averting a possible attack for the person to remain quite still and allow the dog to sniff and investigate. This is part of the normal "good manners" of a dog and if people realize this, they can certainly reduce the number of cases of people being bitten by dogs. It is

During social investigations, one dog will stand still, present its groin and allow another dog to sniff.

Dogs instinctively respond to various body regions during social investigation. Here a dog is duped into sniffing the rear of a dog-shaped statue.

Photos courtesy HSUS

sudden movement that makes a dog attack, and the most fatal thing that a dog or person can do is to move suddenly or to attempt to run away when confronted with or challenged by an aggressive dog. Then one is more likely to be chased and bitten than if one (or one's dog) stands quietly and allows the other animal to approach and investigate.

How does one deal with a dog who shows clear aggressive intent? One could call its bluff and give a direct stare and challenge it, ignore it (since indifference is a form of dominance), talk to it in a quiet, gentle voice or give it a command, hoping that it has been obedience trained, such as "Sit," "Stay" or "Go home." The final resort is to take off one's coat or jacket and wrap it around one's arm to provide some protection. Most dog attacks, however, can be aborted by the person remaining passive and calm. The slightest movement backward, the slightest sign of fear will trigger the aggressive dog to challenge and attack.

I have placed considerable emphasis upon this question of dog bites because an estimated million people are bitten by dogs in the United States each year. This means that something is seriously wrong in the relationship between dogs and people. I feel that many people don't understand dog body language and don't know how to behave around a strange dog. I also believe that a dog that does bite without due cause can be a product of improper breeding, because we do know that bite inhibition is genetically transmitted and is an inherited behavior that should be selected for. Also, a dog that is not raised correctly, is not socially adjusted during its puppyhood to regard people as dominant "pack" leaders as well as loving parents, can grow up to be a social delinquent that has no qualms about biting anybody. Overindulgent, permissive rearing generally results in such a dog.

Another aspect of dog bites should be emphasized, what I call the "biological accident," as for example when a dog misinterprets the sudden approach of a child as a threat when the dog is eating. A jogger or bicyclist may not be seen as a human being per se, but as a moving, receding object to be chased. In other words, the sneakers or bicycle could be perceived by the dog as prey to be chased and bitten. What I advise under such circumstances is for the bicyclist or jogger to stop, turn around, face the dog and talk to it in a normal voice to inform the dog that one is a human being and not simply a stimulus that releases instinctive prey-chasing and biting.

Dog bites could be significantly reduced through proper breeding and improved rearing, and through educating people and children in the way to behave around dogs and to understand whether a dog's intentions are friendly.

Another very important aspect of dog behavior is how animals orient to each other when they are interacting. As you may have often seen, dogs will approach each other side on and will frequently circle before one stands still and allows the other to sniff it. Strange dogs generally avoid a frontal or face to face approach. Frontal approaches occur when animals know each other and there are obvious playful or friendly intentions or when rivals meet. It is very important when approaching and handling a strange dog to avoid direct eye contact and a frontal approach. Handlers and judges at dog shows who approach a strange dog frontally deserve to be bitten when they ignore this important social ritual of approaching sideways as a friendly and respectful canine gesture!

A direct stare, as between two human beings, two dogs or a dog and a human being, can be a challenge and can intimidate an animal into behaving submissively and passively. If you know the dog or are confident about handling it, a direct stare can be a form of very effective social control. It is also essential when disciplining a dog before giving a verbal command to establish eye contact. But with an animal that you are not sure about, avoid challenging it with a direct stare, because it could respond by attacking. While the dominant one will give a direct stare as a challenge, it may also avoid eye contact, not as a sign of submission but as a sign of indifference. It is rather like your saying "Hi" to someone in the morning and their avoiding eye contact and giving you the cold shoulder. This is another way of asserting dominance. It is also one way of averting an attack with a dog who is challenging you—turn away and pretend that the animal is not there. This can be very disconcerting to the dog, who could well interpret your avoidance of eye contact as a sign of confidence and psychological superiority. But beware: to back away and avoid eye contact means fear and submission!

The next psychological key area in dogs is the muzzle. Seizing a dog around the muzzle is a very effective method of control and assertion of dominance. One dog will assert dominance over another by seizing its muzzle or grabbing its shoulder-scruff area and shaking hard. We can mimic these behavior patterns to discipline or control an unruly dog. It is much harder for a dog whose muzzle is being held to open and close its jaws, because of the arrangement of the musculature. Perhaps this is why putting a muzzle on a dog or seizing it firmly around the muzzle is such an effective way of controlling an aggressive animal and asserting dominance over it. The ideal way for an owner or handler to assert dominance over a dog to aid behavioral control is to seize the muzzle in one hand and to grab the scruff of the neck in the other. With larger dogs, of course, this can be risky, but once a muzzle is placed on the animal it is remarkable how its behavior will quickly change from aggression and assertion to submission.

In summary, there are two keys to asserting dominance and control over a dog: the shoulder-scruff region, which can be held or shaken, and the muzzle region, which can be seized and held or muzzled with gauze bandage or other suitable material. There is clearly no need for a person to strike a dog; in fact, hitting a dog in order to dominate or control it is quite unnecessary, and with some breeds, particularly Terriers, could mean aggressive retaliation. Using the psychological judo of the scruff hold, the muzzle hold, eye contact and an appropriate growling voice, one can effectively control most dogs where friendly voice and actions, including groin or inguinal contact and petting, fail to establish rapport.

Submissive dogs engage in face-oriented licking—kissing, if you wish. This behavior is derived from pups soliciting food from the mother, who would normally regurgitate food for them. The theory is that this behavior of food soliciting persists into maturity as face-oriented licking. It would be very interesting to see what an adult dog would do when kissing its owner if the owner were to suddenly regurgitate half his dinner!

Other intriguing aspects of dog behavior can give us a deeper appreciation of dog psychology. For example, dogs will mark trees and fire hydrants: this is an important social communication ritual. Dogs when out on the leash should be given plenty of time to sniff these scent posts—such behavior is perhaps analogous to a human being's reading the newspaper. Dogs mark trees and other vertical objects not so much to stake out their territory as to leave a calling card. Dogs that are very closely bonded, especially males and females, will carefully mark over where their companions have marked. In cities this social ritual can have a significant environmental impact, affecting the welfare of trees, and may contribute to the death of many young trees. It is also a very potent health hazard for communicable canine diseases, particularly leptospirosis and canine hepatitis.

When a dog has finished marking, it will often scrape the ground with its feet. This is not a rudimentary form of catlike cover-

Scent marking—an important social ritual in the dog's world.

Canids, by nature, enjoy rolling in unusual odors, as this wolf demonstrates when presented with a piece of perfumed tissue paper.   *Photos courtesy HSUS*

ing-up or burying but rather leaves a very clear visual mark to show where the animal has been, much as a leopard, after spraying a tree, will rear up and rake the tree with its claws.

One of the most obnoxious behaviors for many owners is that of the dog when it finds some foul-smelling material. Dogs love to roll in obnoxious organic material because they have such a highly evolved sense of smell, probably a million times better than ours, and I believe that they have an esthetic sense in this modality: they like to wear odors much as we, a more visually oriented species, like to wear bright clothes or something different for a while. Wolves enjoy rolling in meat or some other food they particularly like before they actually eat it. This again may mean that "wearing" certain odors is an esthetic experience, the aroma remaining to be savored long after the meal has been eaten!

The facial expressions of dogs are rich and varied. Few people realize that a dog can express more than one emotion at one time. For example, an aggressive snarl or sneer can be combined with a more fearful expression, in which the lips are pulled back into a submissive grin, these two simultaneously combined expressions being indicative of both fear and aggression—the face of a "fear-biter." Dogs also have a clear open-mouthed "play face" expression, often accompanied by panting, which is the human equivalent of laughter. Try panting at your dog after you have gotten down on all fours into a play bow. Now you are really talking dog and saying "let's play." Domestic dogs also show a complete mimicry of the human grin, in which the lips are retracted vertically. Sometimes this display is misinterpreted by people as an aggressive signal, while in reality the dog is doing nothing more than making a rather toothy greeting grin of its human companions.

It is remarkable how similar much of the body language and many of the facial expressions of dogs and humans are. The better we understand the behavior, emotions and intentions of dogs, the more enriched our relationships with them will be; we will also be able to handle them and communicate with them more easily and above all, through understanding their ways, we will come to appreciate their intrinsic worth as sensitive, intelligent beings.

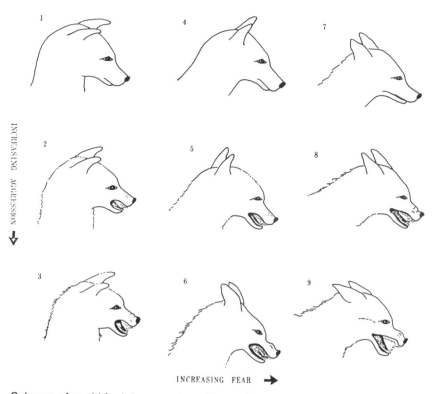

Schema of canid facial expressions illustrating simultaneous and successive combinations. 1-3: Erect ears, small mouth and aggressive pucker (antero-horizontal contraction of the lips) give way to an open mouth threat with vertical retraction of the lips. 4-9: Ear postures shift and the neck is held more horizontally; the submissive "grin" (posterohorizontal contraction of the lips) combines with varying degrees of open mouth threat and vertical retraction of the lips.

Play bow by dog at left is reciprocated by dog at right with an open mouthed, play-face grin.

38

4

How to "Decode" Dog Behavior

THERE ARE other aspects of dog behavior that can be difficult to "decode." What is involved is a careful observation of the animal's behavior and development in all kinds of contexts, to enable one to ascertain what motivates ("turns on") certain behaviors and what the outcome is for the animal of behaving in a certain way.

In decoding dogs' behavior (for example, in understanding why dogs howl at sirens or scrape the ground after evacuating), I have found my studies of wild carnivores—foxes, coyotes, jackals, and wolves—and other research on wild cats, lions, bears and such most helpful. These species are distant cousins of our pets, and an understanding of their behavior allows for an evolutionary, social and ecological perspective, which is essential because some of the behavior of our animal companions is influenced by domestication. (Domestication includes genetic, developmental, social and environmental influences on an animal's behavior.)

VOCALIZATION

Domestication and breeding, for example, have profoundly influenced dogs' ability and proclivity to howl. All wolves howl for a variety of reasons, primarily communication, but not all dogs. Many bark where a wolf would howl. Most dogs, like wolves, do let out a long and plaintive howl when they are alone, lonely and seek contact with packmates or owners. But many dogs confuse their owners when they let loose a volley of howls and yowls when a police or ambulance siren sounds nearby.

This behavior is often misunderstood as somehow protecting the dogs' ears from damage, or as an expression of distress because the noise hurts the dogs' ears. But cats' ears are just as sensitive, yet they never howl and don't run away once they get used to such sounds.

Understanding wolf behavior can help us decode dogs' howling response to sirens (and to harmonicas, flutes and so forth). When one gives a lone-wolf call in the wild in wolf territory, or broadcasts a tape recording of a wolf, wolves that hear the call respond by howling. This implies that it is a natural social response that a siren mimics and that triggers in our dogs the lonely howl of contact. And a dog shut up alone in a yard or in the house with little or no direct contact with its own kind is more likely to respond to even a crude mimic of its species' contact-howl, like a police or ambulance siren.

Wolves sing together, howl-singing being a pack activity, perhaps celebrating their togetherness as well as advertising to other wolves their occupancy of a particular territory. A dog howling, often in perfect harmony, when someone plays a flute, harmonica or other musical instrument is engaging in group singing just as its cousin, the wolf, does.

SCRAPING

Another wolf and dog trait that many people haven't properly decoded is the way in which they scrape the ground after evacuating. This is commonly misinterpreted as the dog's incompletely covering its urine or feces with earth. As cats bury theirs with great care, it might seem that dogs are lazy or that as eminent psychologist B. F. Skinner once wrongly suggested, the dog's behavior is gradually becoming extinguished.

The baby shows no fear of the dog with lips pulled back and teeth bared. Actually, the dog is "smiling" at the infant, although older children and some adults might interpret this as a threatening expression.

Photo courtesy HSUS/Bonnie Smith

Is this an example of animal altruism? Here are two feral Indian pariah dogs. The dog at the left is grooming his sick companion and was seen to drive away flies from her face and the sores on her back. *Photo courtesy HSUS*

When we study the dog's behavior in context, however, its meaning becomes clear. For example, when a rival dog is nearby, the dog will scrape the ground more intensely, not to cover the scent mark of its urine or feces, but to make a more impressive, conspicuous mark on the ground, which points to, and thus advertises, where its personal scent mark is. This is why dogs urinate and often defecate in selected spots in their territory, and will make these deposits more conspicuous by making scrape marks on the ground, which usually point across the trail toward where they have evacuated.

PUZZLING BEHAVIOR

Some behaviors are especially difficult to decode because the signals are ambiguous. These often frighten young children, who should be taught not to fear loud barks when the dog is also looking relaxed, wagging its tail and "grinning" with its lips back in a friendly smile.

Misunderstandings may also result from the animal's behavior occurring out of its natural context. Considering animal behavior in its natural context can help us understand some of the more bizarre and often irritating behavior of our pets.

Grooming

Dogs often nibble their owners, sometimes even painfully. This behavior is easily decoded when we see one dog grooming another, nibbling its companion's fur. Such behavior we can safely interpret as care-giving or altruistic social grooming.

Homing

Knowing more of our companion animals' well-developed sensory abilities, scientists are able to decode other aspects of animals' behavior. Animals, like many humans, are affected by the full moon, during which time there is a greater negative ionization of the atmosphere that makes many of us more active or "charged." Microscopic iron particles in the heads of cats, bees, pigeons and even humans account for the uncanny behavior of navigation, of lost pets being able to find their way home. They have compasses in their heads!

Psychic Behavior

One behavior that science cannot explain, but that we can intuitively appreciate, is the psychic behavior of pets, like that of the dog who suddenly howled at home, according to his master, at the precise time its companion dog was with its mistress at the veterinarian's being euthanized. (See Chapter 7 for more details.)

Unintentional Conditioning

Sometimes we unconsciously condition our pets to behave in certain ways. For example, a lady consulted me over her noisy poodle. The dog barked incessantly at her feet until she picked it up, even though she scolded it verbally and told it to be quiet. Decoding this behavior was easy for an outside observer. The dog had trained the owner to pick it up, rewarding the woman by not barking as soon as it was picked up. And the woman was rewarding the dog for barking by eventually picking it up.

Knowing the natural behavior of animals outside their domesticated contexts, and being able to objectively stand outside one's relationship with the animal have certainly facilitated my ability to decode animals' behavior. And we all have the ability to empathize, to put ourselves in the animal's place, which is as much a prerequisite for good relationships with each other and with animals as it is for the scientific study of animal behavior and for their care in zoos, laboratories and "factory" farms. When we realize that the economy of animals is such that they do not act without good reason, and that unlike us they are almost incapable of concealing their emotions, intentions and desires, we may acquire sufficient respect to really pay attention to what they are trying to tell us, often unintentionally, with the transparent honesty of little children.

LET DOGS KEEP THEIR TAILS

Puppies should keep their tails. This was the conclusion of veterinarians and humanitarians at the 1986 World Society for the Protection of Animals conference in Luxembourg. Many breeds, from Schnauzers and Cocker Spaniels to Dobermans and Rottweilers, have their tails docked or shortened sometime during the first week of life. While this mutilation—like the practice of ear crop-

The ability to decode and interpret natural canine behavior—even in the most domesticated, socialized dog—is central to an understanding of why dogs act and respond to us as they do. *Photo courtesy HSUS*

The practice of tail docking is a very old one and affects a wide variety of dog breeds. The Welsh Terrier shown here is but one of many whose tails are customarily shortened during the first few days after birth. We do it today primarily to follow custom and for cosmetic purposes. *Rudolph W. Tauskey*

ping—is accepted by dog breeders and fanciers, many who really respect dogs, including many breeders and those who show their dogs in competition, are bent on liberating those breeds from the tail-docking practice. Dogs need their tails, which play an important role in their "body language" communication. Veterinarian Dr. Toralf Metveit of Norway reported at this conference that many puppies whose tails are docked suffer later from infections, and some are more prone to posterior hernias because of weakness of the tail muscles. The tail is also important to the dog, he concluded, because it helps maintain balance when jumping and turning quickly, and also helps protect the hind end from flies. So those who really care for dogs should think twice about cutting off puppies' tails and change the "standards" for all breeds subjected to this cruel and unnecessary mutilation.

Even the dog's voice and degree of predisposition toward vocalization has been channeled by man to meet certain needs. This Black and Tan Coonhound is a typical trailing hound that uses its melodious voice to announce the presence of game being pursued or brought to bay. *Frasie*

5

Animals' Sounds Make Sense

DOGS MAKE A VARIETY OF SOUNDS, as do most other animals, that most people think are just so much noise. But when we stop thinking that animals cannot really communicate their wants, feelings and intentions, we begin to listen to them. And when we really listen, we begin to hear what is primarily an emotional language of sound. This is interspersed with specific sounds that have symbolic or objective meaning, such as the alarm bark of some species of monkey signaling the presence of a ground predator, like a human or jaguar, which is quite distinct from the call given when there is an aerial predator such as a monkey-eagle. With one bark, they know they must run up the tree, and with the other, they know they must run down.

Now some academicians, who might profit by stepping out of their intellects and into the real world of the emotions for a moment, insist that animals have no language as we have. Since there is no grammatical structure in animals' sounds, it is claimed that they have no language or linguistic ability per se. But one definition of language, according to *Webster's Dictionary,* is "any means, vocal or other, of expressing or communicating feeling or thought." Another is "the inarticulate sounds by which animals express their feelings."

(Mechanistic scientists studying animal behavior won't like that!) That animal sounds, to our unattuned ears, seem inarticulate does not mean they are unintelligible (or "dumb"), but rather that they are not articulated together into segmental syntax and grammar, as we do with word-sounds. In our language, we can express a stream of multiple images, ideas, desires and feelings. In animals' language, the stream is narrower but no less meaningful, and a spectrum of feelings, desires, images and intentions are expressed.

My own dog Benji is a typical example. As I am writing, he has come up to me panting, with an attentive, anticipatory expression on his face, and his tail is wagging. His panting (a vocal expression, since it is combined with a breathy "haa, haa") tells me he is excited. About what? I look at him and see the friendly anticipation in his face and I know what he wants. The sun is setting and I'm late again getting him his dinner.

Benji was intentionally telling me something. He was "talking" to me in his own distinct, existentially concrete and honest doggy language. But need I put quotation marks around the word *talking* because it is anthropomorphism to infer that Benji can talk? "Talk" by definition means "to communicate by any means, as to talk in signs; to influence, as to induce." To talk also means a "style of speech" and *Webster's* definition of speech is "the faculty of uttering articulate sounds or words to express thoughts."

Benji's communication satisfied all these criteria and his thought was quite obvious. He wanted me to feed him because he was hungry.

Our conversation stopped there. With a human being, I might have discussed what he or she would like to eat. But after all, Benji has little choice. However, he let me know his disapproval by looking back at me after I gave him his food. After he has sniffed over his dinner bowl, if there isn't one of his favorite items, he always gives me an expectant yet resigned look.

If I come out with one of those items, such as a frozen meat and rice cake I often give him, he utters short, low barks, chucking his head up at the same time, signaling me with his head movements to give or throw him the goody. He never gives these sounds at other times, as when I'm throwing a stick or ball for him to catch.

Dogs make a variety of sounds, some "pure" like a bark, others more complex and mixed, like a yelp-bark. All these sounds have various meanings that express the animal's emotional state or intentions. There's some ambiguity, too, because they often give similar sounds in different contexts, like a dog's barking for attention or out of sheer excitement or enjoyment. So it's important to not only listen to what the animal is saying, but also put ourselves in its place to try to ascertain what it wants and what it is feeling.

Common Canine Sounds
"Mew" of puppies—distress, cold, hunger.
"Groan-purr" of puppies—contentment (also in some adult dogs).
Yelp (and longer "yowl")—distress, pain, fear.
Whine—distress, pain, fear, loneliness, seeking attention.
Howl (mournful)—distress, loneliness.
Howl (more melodious)—pleasure, social howl-singing.
Yowl-howl—sociable "talking," especially among sled dog breeds.
Growl—threat, challenge, warning (of danger or to keep away).
Groan—exhaustion, relief from distress.
Snap (of teeth)—defensive or offensive threat.
Bark—threat, alarm or warning, excitement, attention-seeking (often linked with a yelp or whine).
"Bay"—in Beagles and similar hounds "on the scent," a combined bark-yowl.
Pant—excitement, play-soliciting, analogous to human laughter.

Some dogs can mimic human words, such as "out," "hamburger," and "go-go." I would like to hear from readers who have such talking-dog mimics.

I used to think that dogs bark, yap and howl instinctively—without thought or feeling, and not intentionally to communicate anything consciously. They seemed to make these noises automatically, just because they felt a certain way in a particular context. However, there is conscious intent, because these vocal sounds are made only in certain contexts and not in others.

Animals are as aware of context as we are. Perhaps because of their relatively limited language compared to ours, they must be acutely aware of context to avoid ambiguity of signals. For example, a low growl to other dogs at feeding time will repel them, but a low growl when out in the open may well send them running for cover. Both growls are warning signals. They may not be identical: analysis of these sounds with a spectrograph may identify subtle differences not apparent to our ears. The mate-identification calls of sea gulls, for example, all of which sound the same to our ears, have subtle differences in frequency (detectable on an oscilloscope or sonograph) that enable look-alike sea gulls to recognize each other.

Even so, when similar sounds are given in different contexts, the context itself carries information, and an animal, fully aware of its context, can use the same or a similar sound for a totally different purpose. This is the existential quality of animal sounds and language.

In essence, what an animal says vocally and what it does with its body language, plus its awareness of the context in which it is communicating, make up its language. If we can't figure out the context and be of one mind with the animal (for example, realizing why the dog is whining), then all the rest has no meaning. Their language then seems like unintelligible noise and instinctual body motion.

But by living closely with an animal and having a context-related life together, existentially, pet owners and good farmers always know what their animals are saying to them. There's no magic behind understanding animals. But it must seem so when we are so disconnected from reality to the point of not believing that animals have language and can use it to communicate meaningfully to us.

As animals are aware of the context of events, so they are aware of the sequence of events. This awareness we see in their communication with us. When I come home, Benji barks, giving an excited greeting. Then the bark changes, by including the hint of a yelp. Distress, protest? Then he bows and runs toward the gate. He's telling me, after saying "Hi," that he's ready to go to the park.

His yelp-bark gets my attention, then he tells me his intention with his body language. Other dogs often bring their leash with a "woof" that means "Look at me." What follows is a display of intentionality. The animal is demonstrating that it can anticipate some future event and can communicate this very clearly to an animal or human companion.

Intentionality, anticipation and context-awareness form the intelligent substratum that gives meaning to animals' straightforward language of vocal and visual (body, tail and facial) signals.

It is no use trying to understand what these signals mean without being able to empathize with the animal, to put oneself in its place, and through trial and error, attune one's mind to the animal's intentions, expectations and immediate context of the here and now (or just-so-ness of their existential world). Through such learning, we can all come to understand animals better, know what they are

50

Dogs communicate with us through a variety of sounds and body language. In order to better relate to our dogs, we must also be able to interpret the sounds and signals they send us. In doing so, we achieve an enhanced climate of communication and understanding with the animals around us.

saying to us, and respond appropriately. We have to break free of our prejudices (that animals are dumb) and break the habitual mode of looking for meaning within spoken sounds or words only. The meaning of animals' communication is rarely in words as sounds with specific meaning, but more in the broader realm of context and intentionality.

However, there are some sounds that have specific meaning. A dog's deep sigh as it lies down to rest is a sign of relaxed contentment. A piercing yelp or scream is a clear signal of pain or acute distress. It is up to us to find what is evoking such distress, the specific sound demanding that we look at the context in which it is being given. And animals give mixed sounds to convey more than one emotion, like a dog's yelp-bark when he wants to go out to play.

This "language" of dog sounds that I have interpreted functionally can be broken down into these basic categories: to increase or decrease social distance (to threaten or to solicit) and to call for contact, or to maintain close contact (like pups "mewing" together). Our vocal tone, which colors what we are saying, is called paralanguage. It expresses, often unconsciously, what we feel—friendly, aggressive, fearful, solicitous and so forth—and essentially mimics these basic emotional sounds with which animals communicate to each other. Hence, they can understand what we say, to some extent, because it is *how* we say what we say—the emotionality behind the spoken word—rather than what we say that has meaning to them. They aren't so dumb after all, are they!

Sound is a very primal and primitive form of communication, changes in respiration—sudden expiration with alarm (leading to a cough or bark) or relaxed inspiration and expiration (leading to a contentment groan or purr)—being an evolutionary development of auditory communication that gives information to others about one's internal emotional state.

The more we attune our own ears to these primal signals of animals, the more we can understand their emotions and intentions. Such attunement is indeed *at-onement.*

DEBARKING

Some media attention has been given to the issue of debarking dogs. This operation, which is done under a general anesthetic and is painless, entails snipping the dog's vocal cords so that it is unable to give a loud bark. This operation is performed on dogs in research laboratories and other places where they are kept in a confined space and their barking is distressing to people working with them or living nearby. The vocal cords do tend to grow back, so that the operation will need to be repeated at a later date. I personally do not endorse this procedure, especially as a routine, since dogs do use their vocal cords to communicate and to express their intentions and emotions. Even though there seem to be no negative psychological consequences to this procedure, it should certainly not be performed as a routine cosmetic operation. To my mind, it is the last resort before getting rid of the dog following neighbors' complaints that "your dog is making too much noise." Many dogs can be trained not to bark, and those suffering from separation anxiety when left alone can be helped considerably by having a companion dog or cat to live with or simply by being left with a radio or television turned on. More than one dog has rescued its owners from a burning house by barking and awakening them, and certainly a dog's barking is one of the best deterrents to a would-be intruder. So people who are thinking about having their dogs debarked should think twice.

"BREATH-TALKING" IN DOGS

Recent research has discovered that elephants are able to produce very deep sounds, inaudible to the human ear, by vibrating air in the base of their trunks. This is called infra-sound and may be used by elephants as a channel of long-distance communication.

Closer to home we have a mode of close-proximity communication in dogs that I term "breath-talking." The dog doesn't actually vocalize and express the usual repertoire of growls, yelps, whines, howls or barks. Sometimes, however, the vocal cords may be involved to produce a low-frequency groan or sigh. Check out your dog's breath-talk repertoire. When dogs are excited, they will often pant loudly. This is a clear signal often linked with a play-bow and other play-soliciting gestures.

Then there's the slow, deep and very audible exhalation that dogs give when they lie down, which can sometimes sound like a sigh of relief or contentment. Dogs that are enjoying being petted or massaged will frequently give repeated deep exhalations, a clear expression of relaxed pleasure.

When soliciting attention, many dogs make snuffling sounds that puppies make when they are rooting around the mother to find a teat to nurse on. And my own two canine companions usually make snuffly and sneezing sounds when they wake up in the morning and are ready for a treat and a romp outdoors.

This breath-talking is not mere coincidence. Changes in the rate and depth of breathing occur with changes in emotional and motivational states. The more attuned we are to this mode of canine communication, the better we will be able to relate to our canine companions.

TALKING ANIMALS

Truth or fiction, it is thought that in ancient times people could talk to animals and understand them because the animals were able to talk themselves. Native peoples all over the world who live close to nature learn as children to recognize the sounds of animals. A shepherd who was not alerted by the alarm call of a deer or the excited cawing of a raven might lose one of his flock to a lion or wolf.

He learned to listen to what the animals were saying around him, because their various sounds had meaning. Without a knowledge of animal talk, the shepherd would not know when a lamb was lost or in distress, or when his flock sensed danger. Likewise hunters listen to the talk of animals around them, knowing that a sudden alarm call could mean that one or more animals has seen him, while their continuous social babble means that they have not caught sight or scent of him so he can advance even closer. Some hunters even mimic the courtship and social calls of certain prey species, actually talking to the animals to allay their fear and draw them closer.

It is clearly more truth than fiction that people can talk to animals and that animals talk, too. That these abilities were perhaps overblown into some mysterious power or dismissed as folklore or myth by "civilized" people is understandable. Not living close to animals they would not have the opportunity to learn their rudimentary emotional language and certainly would never comprehend animal talk. By listening to the various sounds that animals make, our forefathers had little difficulty in knowing what animals were feeling and likely to be thinking and doing. To one not familiar with animals, this would seem like some incredible power. However, once your ears are attuned to animal talk, along with your emotionality, it is easy to feel and therefore know what they are saying.

Dr. Eugene Morton, with the Smithsonian Institution's National Zoo, has been analyzing animal sounds and finds that when we disregard the words we ordinarily use, our speech patterns follow

Left: In this example of re-directed aggression, one of a pair of coyotes turns and bites its companion to perhaps incite it to attack a stranger (S). Incidents of this kind are common in groups of dogs.

Below: During group play, one dog is often singled out by its companions as the object of a "pack attack." The resulting ganging-up and teasing are almost never serious, and all the dogs, including the "victim," enjoy the game.

Photo courtesy HSUS

the same rules whereby animals talk. For instance, when a person is talking in a friendly voice, as to a pet or baby, the voice pitch increases. Similarly, animals' sounds generally are at a higher pitch and lower intensity when they are being friendly toward each other, tending their young, engaging in courtship or showing submission to a social superior. Whines, whimpers and twittering and purring sounds belong to this category of feeling and intention.

Human speech has a lower pitch when a person is feeling aggressive or is being demanding. Likewise an animal that is asserting its dominance over another or is preparing to attack will emit lower-pitched sounds, from growls to roars. Lizards, birds, dogs and lions all make such sounds, which clearly express how they feel—their motivational state.

Animals can give more complex messages, too, which express more than one emotion and intention. A dog's whining growl expresses both fear and readiness to flee or submit, and aggression and preparedness to attack or defend itself.

High-pitched, high-intensity sounds are part of animal talk associated with alarm, as when a bird or monkey is frightened by a cat or leopard. Humans emit similar sounds when frightened, so it is easy for us to identify and thus empathize with the emotional state of animals who make similar heart- and gut-wrenching sounds.

According to Dr. Morton, the bark that birds, dogs and other animals make is a mixed signal that has high- and low-frequency components. The animal is neither purely aggressive nor purely fearful but is alert and ready to respond to whatever transpires. For instance, a dog that hears a noise outside its immediate territory will bark. Once it sees who or what is making the noise, its bark will change to include growls if it is an intruder, or whines and yelps if it is its owner returning from work. A bark can also be a way of saying "Look at me" or "See what I want," an emphatic way of gaining others' attention, much like a yelp or a whine, though the latter sounds are more solicitous or appeasing. Furthermore, the more excited, alarmed, or distressed an animal is, the more frequently it will repeat a particular sound. Dr. Edwin Gould, curator of the Department of Mammalogy at the National Zoo, sees a similarity between such repetition and pause patterns in human speech. A person's emotional state is reflected in the pattern and timing of pauses, one who is excited having a speech pattern with few pauses.

So if we attune our ears and listen with our hearts, it is not difficult to make sense out of the sounds of animals. And it is not some ancient myth or folklore that animals can talk, and that we can talk to them. Our tone and pitch, like theirs, give meaning to what is felt and express motivational state and intentions. The modern science of animal behavior is confirming what our ancestors knew all along and is also reaffirming our kinship with animals.

It can be said that people who really understand animals—their body language and the ways in which they express their emotions, needs and intentions—are able to talk to them. The importance of such understanding is eloquently expressed by American Indian Chief Dan George:

> *If you talk to the animals*
> *they will talk to you*
> *and you will know each other.*
> *If you do not talk to them*
> *you will not know them.*
> *And what you do not know*
> *you will fear.*
> *What one fears*
> *one destroys.*

Hence, it is important for animals that people understand and respect them, and indeed talk to them, otherwise people will continue to be indifferent toward them and even afraid. What one loves and understands one will not mistreat or destroy.

During a courtship display, an Alaskan Malamute executes a play bow before a wolf. The play bow may be a ritualized and evolved display of relaxation indicating playful intentions.   *Photo courtesy HSUS*

6

Understanding Your Dog's Super Sense—Smell

A DOG'S SENSE OF SMELL is guesstimated to be a hundred thousand times more profound than ours. Relatively speaking, our sense of smell is almost nonexistent, compared to that of a dog.

Perhaps they are more aware than we of the effect different odors can have on their emotions. Odors can make animals fearful, aggressive, sexually aroused or infertile, and can even kill them. In us at most they can evoke sexual arousal and feelings of "edginess"—fear and readiness to flee or fight (as research with perfume pheromones has shown), or security (like a child's familiar-smelling blanket).

Pheromones are fascinating. These are external odors (chemical molecules) that are absorbed when inhaled, stimulating the central nervous system, just as internal hormones do. They can synchronize menstruation in humans and influence estrus or heat in dogs and other mammals.

One of these pheromones, called aldosterone, a breakdown product of testosterone secreted by the testicles, appears in the saliva

of boars when they sniff a receptive "porkette." This saliva pheromone puts the females into a trance so the boar can do anything.
Perfume manufacturers have put this into both men's and women's
toiletries. Yet we secrete our own! A strong odor of aldosterone
generally attracts or repels women and is ignored by men or evokes
"edginess."

All dog owners know how attracted and "turned on" male dogs
are when they sniff the odor of a bitch in heat. The pheromone in
the bitch's urine is so intense to the male that it stimulates his sexual
drive, a behavior that is far less dependent upon olfactory (smell)
cues in humans.

Human society would function very differently if odors so profoundly affected our behavior. I often contemplate the probability
that our evolution necessitated our withdrawing from such potent
influences upon our brains and behavior, so that we could gain
control, objectivity and rationality. If I sniffed as much as my dog
Benji does on our walks, I would never have time to think!

I was bemused, several years ago, when one of my students at
Washington University in St. Louis, where I was a professor of
psychology, recorded "social sniffing-investigation" in a caged pack
of dogs as occurring sometimes hundreds of times a day. Why, I
wondered, should these dogs, who lived together and knew each
other well, have to keep sniffing each other in various places? To stay
in touch, I now conclude. Part of the animal's attunement, indeed
at-onement with its immediate physical and social environment, is
through its sense of smell.

Consider the confusion to pets when their owners come home
smelling of another animal that they have been petting. And reflect
also upon the confusion of our pets at the odor of certain hand and
face creams, lotions and preparations that contain a chemical similar
to the pheromone in the urine of female dogs or that contain farm
animal byproducts that smell like food.

Such profound reactions as sexual arousal and aggression are
not uncommon. They clearly indicate that animals' consciousness of
odors is far more sensitive and responsive than ours. They are also
more dependent cognitively and socially upon contact with this dimension than we.

The heightened sensitivity to, awareness of and dependence on
scent in dogs may be due to the fact that they have extensively
developed nose-receptors and also have a second organ of scent,
which we and other primates lack (so that we can think reflectively?).
This is called the vomeronasal organ, or Jacobson's organ. It is

located in the nasal cavity and has two ducts or canals that open behind the upper front teeth, creating a direct conduit to whatever the animal licks and tastes. This organ connects with the amygdala, a brain center associated with sexual, territorial and aggressive social behavior.

The heightened sense of smell in dogs makes them more aware in this sensory realm than us. For example, tracker dogs can find missing persons from the scent of their possessions and can discriminate between identical human twins on the basis of odor. Trained dogs can smell out hidden guns, bombs and drugs with a speed and alacrity that seems psychic to us spellbound but almost smell-blind humans.

Trained dogs are used by some farmers to help detect when cows are ready to be bred. Other farmers have learned that if they disrupt the normal social environment of pigs by separating the sexes, the absence of the stimulating odor of boars will delay sexual maturity in gilts (young female pigs).

Farmers also know that pheromones influence how a nursing horse or sheep will accept an orphan. The nursing animal is more likely to accept the orphan if it is covered with her odor or with the skin of its own dead offspring. A nursing cat or dog will more readily adopt an orphan—even a baby rabbit, lynx or wolf cub—if the orphan is wiped over with a moist sponge that has been wiped over the mother and her offspring.

Outdoors, dogs urinate and often scrape afterward to leave a "pointer" sign on the ground indicating where they have marked. This is a social ritual, the urine mark indicating, to other dogs, the individual's identity, sexual state and possibly emotional state. Urination-marking in dogs is analogous to singing in birds—it helps the animal protect its territory, attract mates and repel rivals.

Emotional state can be communicated via the sense of smell in animals. People have often wondered if dogs can smell fear. As yet, no research has confirmed this in dogs, but the probability that they can is high. Research has shown that rats become extremely agitated when they smell the air blown over them from a separate group of rats that are reacting fearfully to a threatening stimulus. Fearful dogs often evacuate their anal glands—a terrible odor, which may be an alarm signal to other animals. In the skunk this has evolved into a weapon of defense.

Our emotions do affect our body chemistry and I am sure our pets can and do divine our emotional state, if not our personas, from the odors our bodies produce. The sweet smell of puppies, kittens and

That the dog's sense of smell is extraordinary is common knowledge. Perhaps the most familiar application of canine scenting ability is the work of Blood-hounds in trailing lost persons and fugitives. In recent years, other important uses for the canine nose have been developed, from search and rescue work and bomb detection to identifying cows in estrus.

Photos courtesy HSUS/Dommers

babies is a familiar human experience, sometimes producing a déjà vu experience, since smell can evoke deep emotional memories. Some human and animal doctors regard their sense of smell as an extra, almost intuitive, diagnostic tool.

Rats can detect the difference, on the basis of odor, between strange and familiar caretakers and between schizophrenic and non-schizophrenic people. This means that our personalities and emotional states influence our body chemistry and thus the chemical odors that we produce. Some of these odors are influenced by the kind of food we and animals eat and the kinds of bacteria that live on our and their bodies. Hence differences in odor can be attributed to such external factors rather than to genetic or racial differences. The "prejudice" that dogs often show (as fear or aggression) toward humans of the sex opposite their owners' is more likely due to a different odor related to sex pheromones than to genuine sexual discrimination.

Dogs do get attached to the familiar odor of their master or mistress, and if the latter rarely meets others of the opposite sex, pets may react fearfully toward them or show aggressive reactions I interpret as social rivalry or jealousy. A male dog may cock his leg against a visitor. Putting their own marks on things unfamiliar or intrusive may make animals feel more secure. They will even mark over another's mark, like the dog who urinates on the exact spot where another dog has marked. This could be simply leaving a "calling card" in a communal place, or it could be done to obliterate the other's mark. I have seen dogs of opposite sex out together and often when one marks its mate would mark over the same spot with its urine, possibly signaling to other dogs that they are together.

Since we are unattuned, consciously, to this profound realm of smell, we humans are out of touch cognitively and emotionally with a vast realm of experience. If we can come to appreciate how disconnected we are, and if we can learn, through our pets' behavior and knowledge of animal behavior, to become more consciously connected, we may indeed open up new vistas. The "soul" or essence of many things is expressed in its odor, be it the perfume of a rose or the fresh-baked bready aroma of a puppy's breath or the sweet aroma of a baby's scalp. These essences have a profound effect on animals' behavior, and as research is showing, on our virtually unconscious behavior also. The odor of a strange male mouse can stop a recently mated female mouse from becoming pregnant. And a mouse placed in the cage of one that has previously defeated it may die within a few hours even though the dominant mouse isn't in the cage with it.

Dogs held on a leash tend to be more aggressive than when they have greater freedom to interact with others. In situations where leash restraint is required, caution is needed in social encounters, but social encounters are beneficial for most companion dogs. *Photo courtesy HSUS*

Since animals also enjoy certain odors, we might well wonder just how "high" they can get. Dogs love to roll in obnoxious materials so they can "wear" the odor on their bodies. They have an esthetic dimension to their sense of smell as we have in the visual and auditory modes of perception, enjoying art, color and music. Olaf Stapleton, in his sci-fi book *Sirius,* eloquently described what a mystical experience in the modality of smell might be like for a dog—or a human with a dog's senses. Whatever odors do to our animal companions, we should attempt to attune ourselves to this extraordinarily profound sense and at least give our dogs plenty of time to do their sniffing and marking when they are being walked and are reading the "small print" in their neighborhood newspaper.

Dogs share with other animals the apparent ability to exercise extrasensory perception. Accounts of such incidents, documented and otherwise, are plentiful, and add a special dimension of intrigue to the companion animals which are commonly around us. *Photo courtesy HSUS/Dorothy Carter*

7

Supernature and Psychic Abilities of Dogs and Other Friends

THE AMAZING SENSITIVITY, intelligence and awareness of animals is occasionally revealed in so-called psychic phenomena. These psychic or extrasensory feats of some animals and humans are beyond the realm of contemporary objective scientific inquiry, which reflects a limitation of the scientific mind rather than of science per se.

During the winter of 1961–1962, a man by the name of John Gambill died in a hospital in a town in Texas called Paris. It is documented that at the time of his death, hundreds of wild geese circled the hospital, calling loudly as though in requiem. One would surely regard this as sheer coincidence, yet this man had established a wild goose sanctuary on his farm. The birds somehow seemed to know. The sanctuary had begun years before, when he nursed an injured wild goose back to health. He released the bird, which returned the following fall with twelve other geese and eventually over three thousand wild geese came to spend the winter safely on his property, which he willed to the state as a permanent bird refuge.

This moving anecdote is one of several that have been well-documented in books, newspapers and magazines. I have selected a few that will make you wonder about the inner world of animals; it may also, as it does for me, jolt you into considering the possibility that animals have a different form or dimension of intelligence, a natural, inner wisdom that humans only rarely experience. Some of the following anecdotes explain themselves, and one should not attempt, at least at this stage of our ignorance, to read more into them than what simply happens. A healthy skepticism and an open mind are all that is needed to enjoy these phenomenal accounts.

In his well-researched book, *The Psychic Power of Animals,* author Bill Schul provides some extraordinary accounts of animals' abilities, some even beyond the grave. A man in Kansas City was awakened by his Spaniel's barking and saved his family from a house in flames. The dog had died six months before. A Colorado motorist stopped on a mountain road late at night when he suddenly saw his Collie by the roadside. He found that the road ahead had been washed away and that he would have plunged over a cliff if he had driven on. Yet the Collie had been dead for a year. Schul also reports how bees swarmed over the coffin of their deceased beekeeper in England, then returned to their hives.

Other abilities are no less incredible. A sick mountain goat wandered into a small California town and made her way to the local doctor, who treated her. The following year she returned bringing her sick kid. (I have a report of a bobcat who was rescued from a trap, nursed back to health and returned the following year to show her human friend her litter of cubs.)

Schul also relates how a boy, lost in the wilderness, was kept warm all night by a family of beavers, and how a cow became a "seeing-eye" guide for her blind farmer-owner, who never had to train her.

I have a friend whose genealogy goes back to a very old aristocratic family in Ireland. He tells me that whenever one of the family dies, foxes, which are normally quite secretive during the day, come out into the open and congregate around the ancestral home. There are two other old families in Britain that are similarly linked with foxes, the wild animals appearing, as though to pay homage, when a member of the family dies. What connection, what historical kinship exists between these families and the foxes on their land?

Other old European families believe that the sound of an owl hooting close to the house could mean the imminent death of a relative or close friend. Such totemism, or superstitious belief in an animal that appears at certain times, could be a living fragment from the distant past when we all "read" animals and used them as a source of information. American Indians today claim to be able to derive meaning from the flight patterns and direction of wild geese and from the behavior of a hawk or eagle above them. Perhaps at one time we had a much closer psychic link with our animal kin. Since we were so close to them, living off the land as they did as gatherer hunters, it would be only natural that they might become a source of information, indicators of omens, of things to come. To the "primitive" human mind, the rational link between cause and effect could have seemed vastly different from ours, since to find explanations for certain events, they would look for any correlation or coincidence that seems to fit. The appearance of a raven over a teepee might, by sheer coincidence, have occurred at the time of someone's death. The presence of such a bird subsequently might be interpreted as an omen, and as is often the case, the frequency of occurrence might be greater than would seem due to mere chance. Such coincidences make us ponder the nature of reality and wonder about the link between animal and human awareness.

A journalist friend of mine recently had to have his aging dog, a very close companion, put to sleep. My friend, knowing that this was best for his dog, stood quietly as the veterinarian and his assistant gently held the dog and gave it a painless intravenous anesthetic, from which it would never recover. The dog quickly sank into unconsciousness and then it ceased to breathe. To his surprise, at the moment of death he saw the following: "The dog's lustrous coat suddenly became dull and I saw a silvery shape of my dog rise out of the still body, and then it seemed to diffuse into the air." This is the closest thing that he had ever seen to what he interpreted as a visible aspect of the soul.

While it may seem inconceivable that wild animals such as geese, foxes and ravens can know when a particular person has died, we might be less skeptical of pets demonstrating such ability, considering the close emotional ties of some with their owners. There are, in fact, many documented cases of pets acting strangely—becoming panicked, calling in obvious distress or acting depressed—when someone close to them dies. Such reactions have occurred when the owner, another pet or a family member died. They have also occurred around the moment of death when the sensitive pet is at home and the deceased many miles away. Distance does not seem to prevent some animals from knowing.

It has often been noted that when an elderly husband or wife expires, the spouse may die soon after. The same is true of pets. While in veterinary practice in England, I remember one old lady who died soon after her cat passed away. Coincidence, perhaps? Why, then, should a healthy, hunting Retriever die suddenly after a few days' depression following the death of its beloved companion—a canary? It would seem that in some relationships between both animals and people, the emotional bond in life is so strong that when it is severed by the death of one, the other not only knows and feels, but may also die. I recall a tragic case in which a little boy was in a hospital dying with leukemia. One of his pet pigeons somehow found where he was and perched on the windowsill of his hospital room. He knew which pigeon it was by the identity ring on its leg. The astonished hospital staff allowed bird and boy to stay together—a somewhat less remarkable and therefore more credible case of "knowing" (or what we might call inner wisdom of the animal consciousness). There are several authenticated cases of cats and dogs finding their deceased owner's grave and either visiting the spot once, as though to pay their respects, or repeatedly visiting the grave, sometimes even staying there for years.

Animals will follow their human companions to the grave, and perhaps even beyond. There is another kind of following called psi-trailing, and from the cases that have been thoroughly researched, there can be absolutely no doubt that this phenomenon exists. One of the most celebrated cases was that of Lassie, a mongrel dog who was left behind at a small farm in Kentucky when his owners moved to California. The dog left the people who had adopted him, and months later, he located his family in Pacoima, California. A cat named Clementine made a no less incredible 1,500-mile journey from Dunkirk, New York, to Denver, Colorado, to find her owners. Another cat named Tom holds the distance record of 2,500 miles or more, traveling from the home place in St. Petersburg, Florida, to San Gabriel, California, to find his owners in their new home.

Several years ago when a psychiatrist friend of mine was a teenager, he was given a dog by neighbors who moved from Brooklyn to live in Queens, the adjacent New York county. Alan had had the dog only a couple of days when it ran off. The owners called a few days later saying that they had found their dog walking up and down their new street in Queens and were so amazed, since the dog had never been there before, that they felt they had to keep him after all.

A similar case of psi-trailing was reported on national news in the spring of 1983. A little mongrel dog, left with neighbors in

Colorado, made an incredible journey over the Rockies in the dead of winter and found its owners at their new home in California where the dog had never been.

A young cow called Blackie was recently sold, along with her calf, at an auction in England (*Agscene*, February 1984). The two animals went off to separate farms. That night Blackie escaped and was found the next morning suckling her calf on the farm where her calf had been taken. Her owner was traced via the auction tag that was still stuck on her back. Out of compassion and amazement, she was allowed to stay with her calf. The farms were seven miles apart and Blackie had never been there before. The bellowing of a calf could surely not travel that distance, or its scent, unless cows have remarkable senses. Whether Blackie was psychic or telepathic, or had supersensory abilities, is an open question; but no less remarkable is the strength of her maternal instinct and desire to be with her calf.

One of the most celebrated cases of psi-trailing occurred during the First World War. In 1914, an Irish Terrier named Prince journeyed alone from London, England, and took about two weeks to find his master, Private James Brown, in Armentieres, France, where he was stationed with his battalion.

Without a concrete, physical *explanation* of this psi-trailing ability, many people still remain skeptical even though these animals and others could be definitely identified by their owners. In fact, the evidence for this animal ability is incontrovertible and irrefutable. Even though we cannot explain the hows and whys (except that one of the major whys is love), what does such evidence mean? What is its deeper significance?

It means first that many animals, possibly your pet included, possess mental (or psychic) abilities far more sensitive and better developed than ours. It means that animals may be far more aware of or receptive to another dimension of reality that is relatively closed to us—that is, with the exception of human seers, prophets, clairvoyants and our own occasional flashes of déjà vu and precognition.

The late Dr. J. B. Rhine of Duke University investigated a number of cases of alleged psychic abilities in pets. The following cases leave no doubt that animals possess such abilities. One of the most amazing cases of psi-trailing involved a female dog who was adopted by a family at their summer vacation home. By the end of the summer she had presented them with a litter of pups. They were unable to take the dog and litter back to their New York City apartment so they found a good home for them near their summer

One of the most famous cases of a dog keeping vigil over a grave is that of "Greyfriar's Bobby," a Skye Terrier similar to these. When his companion died in Edinburgh, Scotland in 1858, Bobby watched over the grave for 14 years until his own death. A monument to this dog's amazing loyalty now stands close to where man and dog are now buried.   *Rudolph W. Tauskey*

home. About a month later the dog turned up at their apartment in New York City, an incredible feat, since the dog had never been there before. It was some thirty miles from the vacation cottage. The dog was carrying one of her pups. She deposited it at the feet of her amazed owners and then asked to go out. Several days later she returned with another pup and was off again until she eventually had brought her entire family to the apartment. Happily the people decided to keep her. This story is hard to accept but is one that Dr. Rhine thoroughly investigated and authenticated.

Another of his cases involved a little Terrier named Penny. One and a half years after the death of her mother, a daughter in the family came home to make a visit to the graveyard to pay her respects at her mother's grave. She took Penny with her—the dog had never been there before. While she was freshening up some flowers at the cemetery before going to her mother's grave, Penny got out of her car. To the woman's surprise, when she later went to her mother's grave, there was the dog lying on it, whining pathetically. No other family member had been there for months so it is unlikely that there would have been any familiar scents for the dog to detect.

Two other cases studied by Dr. Rhine clearly show that dogs possess ESP. At the moment his master was injured in an airplane crash, a dog became acutely distressed and crawled and hid under the house. There he stayed for several days, during which time his master lay in a coma at the hospital. The dog finally came out from under the house at the exact time that his master regained consciousness.

A dog in Richmond, Virginia, helped save two boys who were out camping. The dog woke the parents by howling in a very distressed way late at night. The parents felt something was wrong and began to worry about their boys. So they drove out to where the boys were camped, about ten miles away. They found the woods on fire, and the fire was moving toward the sleeping boys' tent. They were able to get the boys out in time, thanks to their dog.

For nearly thirty hours in the spring of 1983, villagers on the island of Minorca searched for a lost three-year-old child, to no avail. Mayor José Tadeo, leader of the search party, returned to his home two miles away, and his two-year-old Irish Setter greeted him but kept whining and scratching at the door to be let out. The man complied, and the dog got him to follow right to the area where people had been searching for the boy. The dog found the semiconscious boy in a small crevice concealed by undergrowth. How could

Another amazing ability dogs possess is psi trailing—finding something or someone in a place they have never been to before or were not near when an event occurred. There does not seem to be a logical explanation for the phenomenon, but there are many documented reports of its use by animals.

Photo courtesy HSUS/Judith Halden

Collies are particularly noted, in fact and fiction, to possess remarkable homing abilities.

the dog have known, since it had been at home, two miles away, all day?

There are ancient documents that tell of a time when some people could "talk" to animals, implying that there was some connection between animal and human consciousness. The later persistence of animal totems, superstitions and such may be remnants of our past kinship in consciousness with animals. How removed have we become, and at how great a loss, as we became civilized and technologized and increasingly alienated from the inner wisdom of the natural world?

The irrefutable evidence of psi-trailing in cats and dogs humbles me and engenders a deeper respect for the seemingly supernatural abilities of such commonplace creatures. Familiarity with them, if it has not bred contempt, has at least fostered an attitude that animals are at least less intelligent than we. Yet by what yardstick do we measure intelligence? The commonplace question "Are cats smarter than dogs?" reflects the ignorance behind our general attitudes toward animals. The answer is that a cat is smarter than a human being—at being a cat. By the same token we demean animal instincts as being something mechanical, reflexlike and unconscious. Take, for example, the ability of migrant species of birds and even butterflies to travel thousands of miles to specific traditional places that they have never been to before. Even when science explains these migratory abilities as being cued by the positions of the sun, moon and stars and by geomagnetic influences, we must wonder still at how such intelligence is inherited.

The most thoroughly researched and publicized case of homing in a pet was of a Collie named Bobbie. He was lost in Indiana and his owners had to return to their home in Silverton, Oregon, without him. Somehow he was able to find his way home, some three thousand miles, in midwinter. This dog's feat was sufficiently well publicized that people who had given him food and shelter on his long journey home made themselves known. This way, the route taken by the dog was approximately reconstructed.

While we can accept the evidence of animals' abilities to navigate and either find their way home or migrate to some distant place, and while we can also credit that some animals can psi-trail, we would surely balk at the suggestion that animals may have clairvoyance—that they can see into the future.

During the Second World War, house cats gained a new respect and appreciation in England for their seemingly psychic ability to sense if a bomb or "doodlebug" missile was going to fall too close for safety. Owners would relax while the air-raid sirens wailed and seek shelter only if and when their cats became agitated. Scientists in China and the United States are attempting to determine how animals, including pets and zoo animals, are able to sense the advent of an earthquake, sometimes days before its occurrence. Physical explanations, such as the ability to detect prequake shifts in the earth's magnetic field, may be forthcoming. Then such sensitivity would have a physical explanation and would no longer be regarded as "psychic."

I believe (but I still need the evidence to prove it) that feelings, particularly those of love, fear and the sadness of loss, can be sensed; that they, like ideas and mental images, affect a sensitive, receptive mind just as physical vibrations of touch, light and sound affect our senses. Animals are generally more sensitive and finely tuned, so to speak, and have a greater ability to detect slight physical shifts in their sensory field of smell, sight, sound and touch (including ground vibrations). Perhaps they are also sensitive to emotional or psychic changes in their sensory field that to us less sensitive beings are relatively supra- or extrasensory. A bee can see ultraviolet light and a cat can hear the ultrasonic squeaks of mice, but we are blind and deaf to both these extremes of the physical field of our senses. The same may be true of the nonphysical or metaphysical realm, except during those fleeting moments when we are relaxed, meditating or going to sleep: when we are not thinking, but are briefly quiet, open and receptive. I like to speculate that millennia ago, when our lives (and minds) were more emotionally attuned, and when we were less preoccupied with planning, rehearsing and reminiscing—in other words, with thinking and talking in our heads to ourselves—we were once free to commune empathically with other animals, as they may well do with each other today, and "know" intuitively, or psychically, as such knowledge is called today.

I have presented a few anecdotes about some of the wonders and mysteries of animals. What remarkable abilities some have demonstrated in their close affection for people. Irrespective of logical explanation or mystical speculation, the fact remains that animals are not dumb creatures living in a twilight world of partial awareness. Nor are they unfeeling, instinctive machines. Suffice it to say that if there is a life hereafter and we continue to demean them and treat them without compassion and respect, then there will be an accounting. And if there is no life hereafter, let us open our hearts and minds to them, for they will indeed enrich our lives, sometimes with more than love and companionship. They may open the door for us to a different reality, the natural, phenomenal world, of which we, because of our state of mind and life-styles, are no longer a part. We are more ignorant than they, in this respect, as so often we are more ignorant of our pets than they are of us!

An essential ingredient in many of the remarkable "psychic" feats of animals is love: their strong emotional attachment to their owners. The importance of proper rearing and socialization early in life, which help establish a strong emotional bond, will be discussed in the following chapters.

DEATH AND GOD AWARENESS IN ANIMALS?

A very experienced dog owner in my neighborhood recently lost her old dog Peanuts. He was in a coma for three days, during which time his old mate, Suzy, wouldn't come into the house. When he died, all five surviving dogs entered the room: the other four consisted of a lost dog the good lady had adopted and her three now adult pups. (The litter was a surprise.) All five dogs approached Peanuts's body, did not sniff or greet him (as they often did), and sat down around him in a semicircle. "It was just like a wake, an Irish wake . . . I couldn't believe it," the woman told me.

Many animals seem aware of death, and though they are less preoccupied by the fear of it than humans, they must sense it and experience grief—emotional separation and loss.

Some believe that such awareness brings with it the glimmerings of religious inclinations and spiritual awakening. Have animals a conception of divinity, or are we the lesser gods of dogs and other creatures under our dominion? I believe this is so and that we must act as gods—with compassion, respect and understanding toward our "sister and brother" animals, as the American native peoples like to say.

Plato and Pythagoras, like Albert Schweitzer and Mahatma Gandhi, would have cautioned that if we abuse our power of dominion and demean or exploit animals unethically, or flatly deny our kinship, then we also deny our kinship with God, and assume dominion over the Creator. This is the sin of *hubris.*

My neighbor's experience with her dogs helped her deal with her grief, for in the dogs' behavior, she sensed and acknowledged her kinship with the dogs in the shared experience of emotional separation and loss. We are indeed not alone. As Saint Paul said, "The whole of creation groaneth and travaileth until now." And what is this "now," but the here and now to recognize our kinship with all life—and our humane responsibilities toward all creatures under our dominion: what Albert Schweitzer called reverence for all life.

But *do* animals have any religious sense? Charles Darwin emphasized that the mental differences between man and the higher animals was not one of kind but of one of degree, and that intelligence, language and religion were not uniquely human attributes. He recognized the body postures and sounds of animals as their language, observed that dogs have a conscience and saw their moral sense and deep affection and loyalty for their owners as approaching religious devotion. Anthropomorphic as this may seem, that the master is to the dog what God is to man is an analogy that poets and others have often recognized and eulogized. J. A. Boone, in *Kinship with All Life,* describes how the shepherd dog Strongheart takes him to a particular place to simply sit and contemplate Nature, a meditative state of being-in-awareness that could be interpreted as a religious experience that he shared with the dog.

8

Raising a Super Pet

THERE ARE three critical factors to consider in the raising of a "super pet." These are termed *socialization, environmental enrichment,* and *early handling.* There is a so-called critical socialization period that is the best time to acquire a puppy, whether it is to be kept as a companion or trained as a working dog. Research studies have shown that a pup most readily "bonds" to people when it is between six and eight weeks old.

SOCIALIZATION

Socialization makes the animal emotionally attached to you which will make it more trainable. If socialization is delayed, say until three or four months or even older, as sometimes happens, the pup will not be sufficiently bonded to you to make him readily trainable. Also, this *primary* bond between the owner and the dog must be well established during this early critical period for the *secondary* bond (liking and trusting other people as well) to develop.

Socialization consists of many important forms of interaction between the young animal and its owner. The process is essentially the same for all young animals, including cage birds (such as parakeets and parrots), cage mammals (rats, gerbils and hamsters), cats, dogs, horses, sheep and other livestock. To some extent, socialization also takes place in such creatures as snakes and other reptiles like turtles and lizards: they become habituated to human handling and lose their fear of people.

Socialization first involves *exposure* to humans so that the young animal becomes accustomed to human presence and to the behavior, sight, sounds and smells of people. Second, through regular handling, they become accustomed to being held, restrained and carried. Those species that are *contact species* and naturally enjoy being licked, groomed or preened by their own kind will learn to enjoy being stroked or petted by a human being. But for an unsocialized animal, human contact evokes fear and avoidance.

Early exposure to the human touch (and to quiet "grooming-talking") establishes a *pleasure bond,* so that later in life the puppy will enjoy and regard as a reward a stroke or kind word of praise from its owner. Petting produces a marked decrease in heart rate, which is a sign of general parasympathetic nervous system stimulation. It is through such stimulation that the pleasure bond and social attachment with an alien species (in this context, with humans) can be established early in life.

Socialization includes other modes of interaction. Care-taking, providing food, water, shelter and security, are essential *parenting* functions. They mimic the activities of the infant animal's natural parent, so that the animal becomes attached to and dependent upon its human foster parent.

As a natural parent may sometimes play with, explore and discipline its offspring, so the human "parent" should engage in such activities. Regular games and romps, tugs of war, hide and seek and play-fighting are bonding activities: those who play together, stay together. Exploring the environment is an essential part of growing up. With the security and instruction of the natural parent, the young animal learns about its environment and through observational learning acquires knowledge from the parent essential for its survival, such as where to hunt or find a safe hiding place. The human foster parent should do no less with a puppy. An animal kept all the time in a cage or kennel will be relatively experientially and environmentally deprived. Its early curiosity *(neophilia)* about novel objects, which naturally leads it to explore its world and so acquire knowledge, will be inhibited by fear of the unfamiliar *(neophobia)*. Early environmental enrichment—providing paced increments of experience by exposing the young animal to all kinds of novel stimuli under a protective parental eye—is part of the socialization process. Within

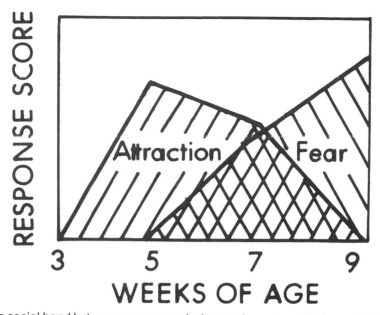

The social bond between a puppy and a human is most readily formed during the attraction phase—between five and eight weeks. If human contact is withheld until a puppy is nine or ten weeks or older, the puppy will be fearful and difficult to socialize.

Courtesy HSUS

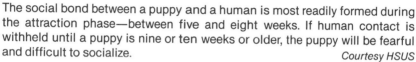
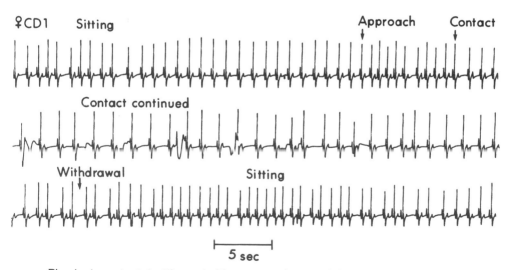

Physical contact (petting, stroking, grooming, etc.) has a profound effect upon the heart rate of many animals. The heart activity charted here is that of a dog. Slowing of the heart is an indication of the generalized effect of touch on the entire nervous system.

Courtesy HSUS

the security provided by the parent, the infant individuates and gains its independence. Overprotective parenting—not allowing the animal to investigate unfamiliar situations and objects, whether innocuous or potentially dangerous—can be as bad as raising the animal (or child) in a restricted environment.

Discipline is the other essential aspect of optimal socialization. Most mammals will discipline their offspring when they step out of line, biting too hard during play, or not respecting the social status of their parents and the "rights" of others.* It is through effective parental discipline that a socially well-adjusted individual develops. Overindulgence and permissive rearing is all too common in pet owners, and usually results in a dog who is disobedient, always gets its own way, and does not take well to corrective training as an adult.

In good animal (and human) parenting, there is a subtle balance between discipline and affection: the latter is not conditional upon conformity, although good behavior may be rewarded with affection. There is also a subtle balance between parental protectiveness, infantile dependence and maturing independence. Overprotectiveness can interfere with individuation/independence, and the denial of autonomy will limit the development of intelligence.

The basic temperament of the animal can be improved through optimal socialization and careful handling. For example, a pup with a timid disposition, if correctly handled, could be helped to become a more stable and adaptable animal by "buffering the genotype."

The earlier such pups can be identified, the sooner they can be helped. A person used to handling pups only a few days old can "feel" differences between littermates. Potentially timid, unstable pups are tense while being handled and may vocalize distress when gently turned over. Once disturbed, they will take longer to settle down than more stable littermates. A stethoscope can be a great help; unstable pups as young as three or four days of age generally have a *slower* resting heart rate than their littermates, the most outgoing of which as a rule have higher resting rates.

If the pup is taken from its mother too early, say between the fourth and fifth week, it can become too people-oriented, and this also can lead to problems, such as fear or aggression toward its own kind, and even refusal to breed.

---

*"Rights" include the right to sleep in a certain place, to be left alone (that is, to privacy), to eat in peace—rights that are often not respected by owners or by their children.

Proper socialization means the difference between a well adjusted, people-loving puppy and a cringing, fearful animal not able to live happily with people. Ample exposure to and interaction with a wide variety of humans from birth on will result in a puppy that is always a pleasure.

ENVIRONMENTAL ENRICHMENT

Some breeding kennels will give puppies lots of human contact, which is a good policy. A puppy with a sound temperament, given plenty of human contact, may then be taken at twelve to sixteen weeks and have only minor problems bonding to its new owner. However, another problem can arise if the puppy is not taken out of the kennel a lot, to a variety of places, especially between seven and ten weeks of age. It may become "kennel shy." I have seen many dogs who have had plenty of socialization to people, but have not had what I call *environmental enrichment.* There is a critical period between five and ten weeks for socialization to people, and there is also a critical period, from the seventh to the tenth week, for learning to cope with unfamiliar environments and novel stimuli. Any puppy kept cooped up in a cage, kennel or house, especially between seven and ten weeks of age, will often show fear when taken into unfamiliar environments or situations.

With an especially outgoing puppy, one with a stable temperament, recovery from this early deprivation is usually rapid if it is not kept confined more than three or four months. But with an innately timid or fearful dog, it may be very difficult, or even impossible, to cure this condition. This problem can be prevented. I advise people with a young puppy (as soon as it has received protective vaccinations) to take the puppy out with them everywhere they go, into all sorts of situations, in the car, into the field and so forth, and to introduce them to as many different people as possible. The puppy's experience of the world must be allowed to expand naturally between the fifth and tenth weeks, otherwise its potential may be thwarted. A pup that is afraid of novel things will be difficult to handle in strange situations and will be a poor learner. Its IQ will suffer because it will be too afraid to explore and investigate new things and learn in the process.

EARLY HANDLING

There are benefits to be derived from *early handling,* which can begin at birth. This entails simply picking the puppy up, repeatedly turning it around and upside down and stroking it for a few minutes every day. The pup can also be placed for one or two minutes on a cold surface (a linoleum floor is ideal) to arouse it and to induce very mild stress. With this early handling from birth to four weeks of age,

Proper handling is basic to proper socialization. The puppy must come to know that the human touch is a good thing. Puppies should be handled from birth, and the handling should be nurturing and reassuring at all times.

accompanied by a little stress, you can produce a dog that is physiologically more resistant to stress in later life.

THINGS TO AVOID

We have discussed what *should* be done during the early critical weeks of development. Now to detail what should *not* be done during this period.

In order to avoid extreme fearfulness and submissiveness, it is important at this time not to be too controlling with the puppy. Training should be done with a very light touch. In particular, *no* disciplinary training should be done between the eighth and tenth weeks, since this is a very sensitive period in a puppy's life. The eighth week is an especially sensitive time, because this is when puppies are most likely to develop an avoidance response if subjected to physical or psychological trauma. The aim at this time should be to give the puppy a sense of confidence and *control.* Puppies develop a sense of control and mastery over their environment when they are given a chance to play, explore and learn. When they are kept in a cage all the time, where they are provided with creature needs but little chance for social interaction, they are in a totally controlled and controlling environment. In such an environment they don't develop a sense of confidence.

And when a dog is afraid of new experiences, he is not going to learn. Fear gets in the way of learning and greatly limits the animal's potential. Since the eighth week is a particularly sensitive time, in that frightening experiences then can have lasting effects, it is obviously not wise to crop puppies' ears at this time. (Ideally, this practice should be abolished.) Also, puppies should not be transported long distances at this age.

There are some other special socialization problems that we need to consider. Pups raised by women can become afraid of men. Pups not raised with their own kind or denied opportunity to interact socially with them may become fearful and aggressive toward other dogs. Dogs who do not have contact with children during the socialization period may be difficult to handle around children later.

The basic lesson is that during the socialization period, broadly defined as extending from the first through the third month of life, puppies should be exposed to all sorts of positive experiences and all sorts of people, while taking care to avoid threatening or stressful experiences, especially during the second month.

SHYNESS

There are different kinds of shyness that must be recognized before an appropriate way of dealing with the problem can be tried out. First, we must distinguish between shyness and aloofness. Many dogs that are extremely friendly, attentive and responsive as puppies become more standoffish and independent as they mature. This is a quite natural phenomenon and shows that animals do have personalities that take time to mature, just as ours do.

Some dogs, however, as they mature become increasingly fearful of strangers and hide when strangers come (be they people or other animals). Yet they are never this way with their owners. This kind of shyness is very common in dogs who spend most of their time indoors and rarely meet other animals or people.

Such animals should not be forced to make friends. This will only frighten them and make things worse. My advice is to let them be. However, if a new person (spouse or friend) or another cat or dog is coming to live in the house permanently, steps must be taken to help the shy dog overcome its fear. Putting a little of the *same* perfume or aftershave on people's hands and ankles and animals' heads and backs sometimes helps, since it is the stranger's odor that often triggers alarm in shy dogs. A few dabs every day for seven to ten days is worth a try if the dog hasn't started to show signs of accepting the human or animal newcomer during their first ten to fourteen days together.

Shyness in dogs can be inherited. So one of the best preventives is not to breed and produce puppies from shy parents.

Some puppies are by nature on the shy side. One way of helping them to become more extroverted and to gain self-confidence is to play with them frequently. A tug of war with an old sock or piece of towel will make many pups more responsive and outgoing. And a regular grooming—even a massage, as I describe in my book *The Healing Touch*—for all puppies will help prevent shyness later in life because such contact establishes a bond of affection and trust.

The above socialization, environmental enrichment and early handling procedures are the three golden rules in creating a super pet. This is not meant to imply that it is possible to improve upon nature, but rather that, by bringing out the best qualities and buffering or compensating for negative attributes, one may create an adaptable and intelligent animal. Studies with infant rats, kittens and dogs given socialization, enrichment and early handling have shown the following attributes: greater resistance to physical and emotional

Unless desirable behavior patterns are inherited, or socialization during puppy-hood neglected, shyness should not be a problem. An aloof or protective nature, as would be typical of this tolerant Chesapeake Bay Retriever, should not be taken as a sign of shy or unstable behavior.

stress; increased resistance to several diseases, including leukemia and induced cancer; enhanced learning abilities because of greater emotional stability; and a more outgoing character, which means the animal is more likely to be highly inquisitive and exploratory and therefore more likely to learn.

SOME GENERAL EFFECTS OF DOMESTICATION

The brains of our pets are smaller than those of their wild counterparts. Generations of domestication and being raised in a relatively unstimulating environment in cage, house or suburban yard have resulted in a reduction in brain size and intelligence in our pets.

Over a hundred years ago, Charles Darwin observed that the domesticated rabbit has a much smaller brain than a wild rabbit, which he interpreted as due to a deprivation of natural outlets for the development of normal instincts and behavior patterns.

More recently, scientists have demonstrated that laboratory rats will have smaller brains and be poorer learners than littermates raised together in enclosures "enriched" with novel toys and manipulation.

It is known that wolves have an average brain size one sixth larger than that of dogs of the same physical proportions, again confirming that domestication can have a marked influence on brain development.

Rats, mice, dogs and captive-raised monkeys, if provided with a rich and varied environment as they are maturing, will be better problem solvers—that is, more intelligent—later in life. Wild and domesticated strains of rats, born and raised under the same conditions, show marked differences in behavior and intelligence. Wild rats, even when bred in captivity, show more complex behavior and are better learners than the bland white rats who have been domesticated over hundreds of generations of selective breeding for docility.

What these studies disclose is that two interrelated processes are involved in the gradual decline in brain size and intelligence in our domesticated companion animals.

First, in a relatively protected domestic environment, there is a relaxation of natural selection pressures that favor intelligence and alertness. A domestic pet need not be intelligent to survive, while in the wild the unintelligent, the poor learners and the unalert would not live long. Nor would their attributes be likely to be passed on to any offspring, since they would die before they reached sexual maturity.

In the more protective domestic environment, natural selection for survival-enhancing behaviors is reduced, and there has been a greater emphasis placed upon tractability, docility and submissiveness toward humans. The general levels of alertness, activity and curiosity (especially arousal by novel stimuli) have also been reduced—in some dogs, to the point of making them "sweet nothings" that are relatively insensitive to or unaware of much that is going on around them.

While there has not perhaps been a deliberate attempt to lower intelligence in domesticating animals, in selecting for a more docile and easygoing animal, arousability, alertness and curiosity may be so reduced that the animal learns very little except when instructed or trained.

Neophilia and neophobia—curiosity and fear of novel stimuli and unfamiliar events—are qualities of the wild animal. They are related to the animal's general state of arousal and attentiveness. No one wants a relatively hyperactive and hyperalert dog that must explore everything new in its environment or flee from anything unfamiliar and intimidating.

In breeding out or reducing these "wild" traits, the domestic pet is made easier to handle and control, but since it is not going to explore its environment with the intensity and thoroughness of its wild counterparts, it will acquire less knowledge. Its IQ will be low as a result of selective breeding for desirable domestic qualities.

A second reason many pets have low IQs is that they are raised in a relatively bland, understimulating and monotonously predictable environment. Life in a cage, a small apartment or a suburban backyard can be so experientially depriving that the animal's potential is never fully developed.

In addition to varying degrees of experiential and environmental deprivation, emotional influences can also get in the way and further restrict the animal in learning new things and, therefore, developing its IQ. These same emotional and motivational influences can also interfere with IQ tests and "educational enrichment." An animal that is afraid or anxious will not perform well. Similarly, one that is basically timid, or too headstrong or not sufficiently motivated by hunger or curiosity (depending upon the nature of the test) may also show an inferior performance.

Aside from carefully breeding dogs to be more alert and out-

Providing a stimulating environment for your dog introduces a natural impetus to an active personality. Too often the effects of domestication translate into a sluggish, indifferent dog that is more a bother than a pleasure.
Photo courtesy HSUS/Bonnie Smith

going to improve their IQs, we can also provide them with a more natural environment, which will help bring out their potential and make their existence more enriched and fulfilling.

In conclusion, raising a puppy is not unlike raising a child. But love alone is not enough. Knowing the developmental stages that your pet goes through and the critical times during its development when special care and attention are needed can help bring out the best in your animal companion.

9

A More Natural Life for Your Dog

AS I DRIVE into the city to work each morning, I often wonder just what is natural anymore. Small parks with their pigeons, starlings and sparrows, smoggy trees and shrubs seem like remote little islands of nature amidst a sea of concrete. Even the parks aren't natural. Many of the birds are alien species, introduced years ago from Europe, and some of the shrubs and trees aren't indigenous to the region either. Yet without its parks, any large city would be even less conducive to our general well-being. The animal in us seems to need a semblance of nature, a facsimile at least, for our psychological well-being. The same is true for our pets. They, like us, have certain instincts and basic needs that can be frustrated if we do not provide some natural outlets for them. Mental and physical well-being are closely linked with how conducive the environment is to satisfying such needs.

Research has shown that if an animal is raised in a deprived environment—for example, in a small cage in a zoo or laboratory—its basic drive to explore and therefore to learn is either inhibited or frustrated. The development of its brain may then be adversely affected by its being raised in a bland, unstimulating environment. Being deprived of various outlets and things to do and to explore, it may become a "zombie," obese, infertile, glassy-eyed and unresponsive, or, because of the deprivation-frustration, it may become hyperactive, pace to and fro in its cage and overreact to any changes in its cage environment or daily routine. If it is caged with other animals, more obvious anomalies may develop, especially when the additional element of crowding stress is evident. Schizophrenialike withdrawal, excessive aggressiveness, infertility and increased susceptibility to certain diseases have been documented in animals kept together with no opportunity to get away from each other for a while. In contrast, animals that are caged alone for extended periods may show signs of social and emotional deprivation and lick or groom themselves excessively, eat or drink excessively, develop stereotyped pacing or running patterns, and even become infertile (because of lack of adequate social and sexual stimulation). Sometimes they will use some object in the cage, such as a piece of food or a water bowl, as a substitute for a sexual partner or for prey to chase and catch, or else they will use one of their own appendages, such as a tail, as something to chase or even to nurse on for comfort, and this may eventually lead to self-mutilation. When a companion animal is introduced to one that has been caged alone for a long time, it may either ignore it or attack it viciously and even kill it. Conversely, because of overattachment, if one caged animal loses its companion, it may go off its food, groom itself excessively and mutilate itself or even die from depression. A mother monkey or ape may become so stimulated by its infant that it grooms it too much and handles it so much that it may die because it never has time to nurse; if it does survive alone in the cage with its mother, they may become overattached and the infant's development toward independence may be retarded.

These extreme examples of what can happen to cage-raised animals in zoos and laboratories may hardly seem relevant to caring for our pets, yet I have seen similar and sometimes identical problems in house pets suffering from the effects of living in an unnatural environment, which can be an apartment (for a dog or cat), an outside pen (for a dog) or a cage (for a bird, hamster or other cage pet). I will describe in detail some of the problems that can arise from keeping a dog in an unstimulating and unnatural environment and also offer several remedies by which the dog's world can be made more natural and therefore more conducive to satisfying its basic needs.

Many of the symptoms seen in captive wild animals are less

There is no mistaking the appearance and actions of a physically healthy dog that is stimulated by an active environment. This robust Norwegian Elkhound personifies the best objectives of dog owning.

obvious and fortunately are sometimes even absent in our pets because of domestication. Through domestication (selective breeding over generations) dogs have become generally more subdued and docile than their wild counterparts. This means, up to a point at least, that they can cope well with a reduced level of stimulation, in that they will not become hyperactive and are less easily bored or frustrated than are captive wild animals. Conversely, when they are stimulated by something novel and unfamiliar, unlike a wild animal they will not usually overreact. Some dogs will not even notice, say, a change in the arrangement of living room furniture or a new tree in the garden, but a wild captive wolf or coyote would notice at once.

While our domestic animals have been tuned down somewhat in contrast to their wild counterparts in order to make them more adaptable as pets, they may still suffer from certain deprivations, and therefore whenever possible we should endeavor to make life as natural as possible for them.

OBESITY

It has been estimated that 30 to 50 percent of our dogs are overweight. This can lead to such complications as circulatory anomalies, heart failure, diabetes, infertility (if they are not already neutered), arthritis and possibly accelerated aging. Steps toward rectifying these problems are part of making your pet's life more natural. This includes a more natural diet and feeding schedule: don't overfeed or feed too often and do not give your dog an excess of table scraps or a diet high in calories. Feed a scientifically formulated complete and balanced diet. Also, provide regular exercise, through play (chasing and retrieving a ball or stick).

JOGGING WITH YOUR DOG

Dogs, like their owners, need and enjoy physical activity, and jogging with your dog can be beneficial. First, have the veterinarian give your dog a physical—older dogs and those with heart disease or chronic lameness should not be subjected to strenuous exercise. Here are some practical tips for your healthy dog-jogging companion.

Jogging with your dog provides both of you with physical and emotional dividends. As a precaution, get your dog a thorough physical before embarking on a jogging program and observe some common-sense cautions when you jog together.   *Photo courtesy HSUS/Sumner W. Fowler, Marin Humane Society*

- Don't push the dog too hard on very hot and humid days—he may get heat stroke. A slow mile or two should be enough.
- Before you jog, let your dog do his thing first—sniff and urine-mark for a while—or he will want to keep stopping and will disrupt your run.
- Train him on the leash to "heel" and trot by your side (not behind you or you might lose him if he stops later when he's not on the leash). A sharp "No" and a tug on the leash will quickly condition him not to keep stopping to sniff and mark all the time. But you must stop first before giving the command. Don't keep running and tug your dog after you, since you could injure his neck.
- Be patient. You will trip over leash and dog, and may injure yourself and the dog, if you keep on jogging when the dog stops to sniff.
- My personal choice is to be prepared for your dog to stop at times and to let him do his thing while you jog patiently in place until he is finished.
- I don't like to see people out jogging with their dogs off the leash unless the dog is extremely well trained and won't chase other dogs or bitches in heat. Few dogs are so well behaved or predictable as to remain close by one's side at all times.
- Once your dog has been leash-trained to jog with you and is obedient, you could try him off-leash, but please, not along the highway or in neighborhoods where you run through or past the territories of other dogs.
- Don't jog your dog too long and too fast at first, especially on sharp gravel surfaces, since this will hurt the dog's soft pads. Be sure your dog's toenails are trim so they don't get torn as your dog runs with you. Also look out for hot tarmac surfaces in summer and salted roads and sidewalks in winter, all of which will damage your dog's feet.

BASIC DRIVES AND INSTINCTS

Much can be done to make life more natural for your dog once its basic needs and instincts are understood. By the same token, life will be much easier for you, since coping with a frustrated pet can be difficult and having a naturally behaving pet can be an enjoyable and educational experience.

First, the basic sex drive, especially in males, needs consideration. Generally dogs adapt better when they are neutered and in a way such treatment is in fact making life more natural for them, because in domesticating dogs we have increased their sex drive. Male wild cats, wolves and other canids only produce sperm during a short one- to two-month period each year, while our pet dogs and cats are constantly potent. It is more "natural," therefore, to have them neutered, and they will be less sexually frustrated and will not want to go out and roam the neighborhood to find mates and to fight with rival males.

The hunting instinct is another deeply ingrained behavior that is frequently frustrated. Dogs will chase cars, cyclists, joggers and even running children as substitute outlets for their hunting drive. The remedy here is frequent play sessions with suitable prey-substitute toys for the dog to catch and "kill." It takes only a little time and imagination for one to come up with appropriate toys to keep a dog happy and active in this regard. Many dogs also enjoy carrying their "prey" around with them, collecting and hiding them in various parts of the house. Be careful, though: if you have a female dog who goes into false pregnancy, one of these prey-substitute toys could become a puppy-substitute, which she may guard and covetously attempt even to nurse.

There is nothing more pathetic than an obese, understimulated pet that is simply given food and water as needed and nothing else. If we treat them with the indifference with which we treat our potted plants, they may well become as unresponsive, dull and uninteresting as vegetables. We owe it to them to cater to their basic needs and to make life as natural for them as we can. There is a condition recognized by veterinarians as the "purebred dog syndrome," in which the dog, usually a purebred animal, simply lies around—an unresponsive object. This could be the final product of domestication, of breeding and rearing our pets to be quiet and docile ornaments. Ironically, some of these animals seem to be mirror images of their owners and of the owner's children too!

Some families that I have counseled about their pets fall into different categories still: the controllers and the permissive indulgers. They either completely control and inhibit all natural behavior in their pets and their children alike, or allow anything to go on, so that both pets and children are unruly and socially irresponsible. There is another category that is quite prevalent: parents and pet owners who ignore their children or pets for long periods and then over-stimulate them with excessive attention and overindulgence. Such inconsistency creates pets that are often confused, unpredictable, emotionally unstable and sometimes hyperactive. Children, too, often mirror such unnatural care. The healthiest and best-adjusted pets and children come from those families in which life is made as natural as possible for children and animals alike. The parents/owners do not overindulge or discipline inconsistently. They are loving and consistent in their behavior and understanding of the needs of those in their care. Catering to the needs of a dog and endeavoring to make its life as natural as possible, just as for a child, does not mean allowing it to run wild or to rule the household. Its needs and rights, too, must be consonant with the needs and rights of others in the family and in the community, responsible parenting and responsible pet ownership being synonymous. Also, the pet must at times be protected from itself, since its natural instincts could get it into trouble. For example, an inquisitive puppy could bite through an extension cord and be electrocuted.

Remember, the more natural you can make life for your pet, the more natural that pet will be. Consequently, it will be a more alert and interesting companion. By making life more natural for your pet, you will also help satisfy some of its basic needs and avoid frustrating others. In so doing, you will encourage the development of your dog's natural potential, which in turn will increase your dog's IQ, because the more stimulating the environment is, the more your dog will respond and learn.

OUTDOOR LIVING FOR DOGS

For various reasons, some people like to keep their dogs out-doors and not make them indoor pets. While one of the most common forms of animal cruelty is to keep a dog outdoors in the yard on a chain at all times, outdoor life for a dog can be a satisfactory arrangement, but not without careful consideration and some invest-ment in adequate facilities.

The larger the enclosure for the dog the better. The floor of the pen should be of concrete or graded gravel, with large chips overlaid with a good six inches of smaller chips and a further three inches of pea-gravel. (Sharp, flinty chips will hurt the dog's paws.) This is necessary to control worms that build up on a dirt-based enclosure,

Left: The healthiest and best-adjusted pets and children come from homes where life for the animals and youngsters Is made as natural as the life style will allow.

Photo courtesy HSUS/Adler

Below: This boy and his Collie companions truly mirror the joy of living they share. Happy dogs have a zest for living and the emotional stability to handle whatever life brings them. Thoughtful, natural rearing and a stimulating environment play a large part in this.

Photo courtesy HSUS/Kellners Photo Service

which is less easily cleaned. All feces should be cleaned up every day to prevent any buildup.

Each dog should have its own kennel or nest-box, which should be well insulated, especially in colder climates. Insulation material sandwiched between two sheets of one-inch marine plywood for the floor, walls and roof makes for a good structure. Since dogs often like to lie on top of the kennel, it should have a flat roof. A sheet of plywood or tarp should be fixed over the kennel, firmly anchored to the top edge of the enclosure to provide shade and shelter. Ideally the opening of the kennel, which should be just large enough for the dog to enter in order to minimize drafts, should face south. The kennel should be set up on blocks a few inches above the ground to prevent water-rot and give extra insulation, and an old blanket or straw put inside for extra comfort.

Food and water bowls can be clamped onto the inside of the enclosure to prevent spilling, at a height low enough for the dogs to drink and eat in a normal, head-down position.

It is especially important in hot weather to insure that there is always an adequate supply of water. In winter, fresh water may be needed three or four times a day if the water freezes quickly in the bowl. (Don't use metal bowls in the winter, because the dog's tongue could become frozen onto the metal and then torn as the dog pulls away.)

A healthy outdoor dog should develop a thick winter coat by late fall. Older dogs with poor coats should be taken indoors in very cold weather, or given an insulated coat to wear or an electric heating pad in the kennel.

I consider it cruel to keep a dog in its pen all day without some freedom outside. Some time indoors with the family should be allowed, especially if the dog is alone outside all the time. Keeping a dog, which is a highly social, pack-oriented soul, alone in an enclosure most of the day and all night is inhumane. Ideally, one should have two dogs under such circumstances, and house them together. Dogs kept outdoors often become lonely for human company and bored so they bark excessively. In many neighborhoods such benign neglect is inexcusable and violates others' rights to quiet environs.

PROVIDING A PET FOR THE PET

One of the most common troubles of dogs today, and one that owners often fail to recognize, is that their pets are dull, uninterested

The dog that lives outdoors at all times can also be furnished with a healthful as well as a stimulating environment. A little planning is involved, but the results more than justify the efforts. *Photo courtesy HSUS/Jackson*

in life, generally lethargic and only too often overweight. It seems impossible that such cases could be in any way related to a well-trained dog's suddenly becoming unhousebroken or being dropped off at the animal shelter to be put to sleep because it barked too much or developed into a house wrecker.

The underlying problem or common cause in these cases is lack of companionship. It is not simply human companionship, but the companionship of their own kind that many dogs require. Some pets do quite well living alone all their lives with only humans, but many of these do become overdependent on their owners, and this can lead to a whole set of other problems.

Many pet owners who consult me want to do what's best for their pet and one of the best things that one can do is to attempt to make a dog's domesticated, confined, indoor life as nearly natural as possible. This doesn't mean giving your dog a live rabbit to chase around the house and kill every few days. But it does mean understanding your pet's basic needs and attempting to satisfy them as far as you can. I do not mean such basic needs as the need to go out and roam free, breed indiscriminately and chase and kill live prey. All dogs, at least while they are still young, enjoy the companionship of both people and their own kind. Contact with its own kind means that your pet can really relate and be understood once in a while, since few of us can really "talk" dog and comprehend all our pet's intentions and actions. Being with its own kind means that your pet can develop, actualize, and express its "dogness"—and probably enjoy it, too. Such freedom to be oneself is surely conducive to both physical and psychological well-being for human beings and animals alike.

The longer an animal is kept without sufficient contact with its own kind, the more it will look to humans as a source of satisfaction for many of its basic needs. But since most of us can't behave or think like a dog and since many owners don't really know what basic needs must be satisfied and how, some very serious problems can develop. The pet becomes frustrated or anxious and may subsequently become increasingly nervous and irritable. The older it gets, the more it may show avoidance, fear or aggression toward its own kind. This paradoxical reaction develops when the dog becomes overdependent on its owner and seems either incapable of relating or unmotivated to relate with its own kind. Its own species is no longer a source of enjoyment. This means that with many older pets it's simply too late to attempt to normalize their lives by introducing another cat or dog

The presence of more than one animal in a household provides effective stimulation for all. Growing up around cats is a plus for the environment of a happy, well-adjusted puppy.

Two puppies growing up together provide each other with companionship and trigger more activity and interplay than a puppy raised by itself would experience. Having a pair of young animals can complicate housetraining and other early training efforts, but many feel the ultimate results justify the temporary inconvenience. *Rudolph W. Tauskey*

105

into the home. The older and more set in its ways the dog is and the more humanized it is, the more likely it is to be extremely jealous of or aggressive toward any newcomer.

In my experience in veterinary practice, the healthiest-looking dogs are more likely to be that way not because of their owner's knowledge about pet care but because they have a companion of their own kind to live with. When a puppy is young, it will engage in lots of play. If it doesn't have another cat or dog to play with, it will play by itself, but with less vigor and enthusiasm. Eventually, it may cease playing altogether, a probability enhanced by most owners' inability to play properly with their pet. Two dogs raised together, however, may continue to play until a ripe old age. I also feel that such animals have more vitality, enthusiasm and naturalness than a dog that has been raised alone with people and without sufficient opportunity to be with other dogs and to develop its inner nature. The dog who has a dog companion is often a more satisfying and interesting pet for those people who want dogs to be dogs. They are certainly more entertaining. Many of my clients and their children have hours of enjoyment watching their pets play together and sometimes joining in themselves. Playful pets can also give a home an ambience of easygoing naturalness and good humor, a factor now being recognized by some psychiatrists who are extolling the mental health benefits of owning one or more pets.

I would like to see some hard figures from some of the larger veterinary hospitals to validate my suspicion that a dog is likely to live longer and have a healthier life with fewer health problems if it has a companion of its own kind to live with. Dogs will frequently groom each other. This stimulation results in a decrease in the heart rate of the animal that is being groomed, and probably of the one doing the licking, too. Such a change in heart activity is an indicator of profound physiological changes in the body that are relaxing and highly beneficial, even having potentially a healing function not unlike the laying on of hands, as I describe in *The Healing Touch*. So it is quite conceivable that two dogs living together might be healthier than one living alone.

Since having a companion will make your dog more responsive and reactive, you are more likely to be able to spot when either of your pets is getting sick. The sooner you can recognize the signs of illness, the sooner you will be able to seek veterinary help. This could mean the difference between life and death for your dog.

One of the most common behavior problems in dogs today is

caused by the animal's reaction to being left alone for extended periods, especially when family members are away most of the day at work or school. Some dogs react by barking excessively or by becoming unhousebroken. Others become house wreckers, tearing up drapes, carpets, books and anything they can get their teeth into. Unable to cope with such problems, owners either abandon these unhappy dogs as misfits or surrender them to the local animal shelter, where they are usually destroyed. All such cases could probably have been prevented and some even cured by providing the dog with a companion animal to relieve its boredom, anxiety and loneliness.

Another stressful time for many pets is vacation time, when they have to be put into a kennel or looked after at home by a neighbor. In my experience, dogs fare much better when their owners are away if they have a companion animal of their own kind. Separation depression, refusal to eat and increased susceptibility to disease are all too common in pets put into a boarding kennel. Having two pets instead of one and making sure the two are housed together when they are left greatly reduces the chances of such undesirable consequences.

Sometimes, for many reasons ranging from infirmity to one's life-style or living conditions (such as living in a high-rise apartment), it becomes a near impossibility to provide one's pet with sufficient exercise and interaction with its own kind. So instead of having one small dog, I prescribe two: and that means two and not three, because with three the chances of rivalry developing, with two dogs picking on the third animal, are very real.

It is important to know the basic rules for introducing your dog to a companion of its own kind. First, if your dog is full grown but not too old and set in its ways, you should not get another adult animal as its companion unless it is of the opposite sex. Dogs of the same sex are more likely to fight. But if they are of opposite sex, it is necessary to have the female neutered to prevent unwanted pregnancies. I would also advise neutering the male if it does show signs of sexual frustration after it has been with the neutered female any length of time.

Ideally have your dog meet the newcomer on neutral territory, say in the park or in a neighbor's yard or shed. Then take the pair home. This will help reduce your first dog's feeling of having its territory invaded by a stranger. But your dog may still feel that its close bond with you has been usurped by the newcomer, so be sure to give the former lots of added attention, or jealousy, rivalry fights and terror could reign in your home instead of trust and affection. If you can, take the new animal companion on approval, so to speak, just in case the two don't hit it off well together. Be sure both animals have clean health records and have recently received all the "booster" vaccines your veterinarian says are needed. Dogs usually get on well together soon after they meet but cats can take a while, anywhere from a few days to three or four weeks.

You may wish to get a puppy as the second pet instead of an adult. I have seen remarkable transformations in overweight, middle-aged, dull and "conservative" dogs who take a renewed interest in life once the new, young animal comes into the house. They have something, or more correctly someone, to care for, groom, play with, sleep with and even compete with for food and for their owner's attention, thus adding variety and zest to life. A puppy that has been raised with an adult of its own kind will also tend to be better mannered than one raised exclusively with people, because adult animals do discipline unruly youngsters, who quickly learn to respect their social superiors.

Many people prefer raising a pair of young dogs of around the same age together. Again, it is important to remember some of the basic rules of choosing animals of opposite sexes, which will reduce dominance fights later in life, and to be prepared to have one or ideally both pets neutered as soon as possible.

Some people have raised the concern to me that two animals raised together might be less responsive to their owners. This is true to some extent in some cases. My advice for those who want a more human-dependent, less dog-oriented dog is to get the second pet as a young puppy when the first one is around six months of age. By this age the first pet will be well attached to the owners and will therefore satisfy the owner's need for a more human-dependent pet.

I do not endorse any unnecessary increase in the pet population, which is a cause of considerable concern today. However, the advantages of having two pets instead of one are indeed many and the multiple benefits greatly outweigh any possible drawbacks. All pet owners do have an ethical obligation to endeavor to satisfy their pets' basic needs, and certainly providing them with the companionship of their own kind will do much to meet this obligation.

Two pets are generally better than one and the chances are that our pets will live longer, healthier and happier lives if they are given the companionship of one of their own kind. Probably the best place to find such a companion, either a puppy or a young adult, would be at your local humane society adoption center. This way you will not only be helping your first pet, you will also be saving the life of another animal and providing it with a good home, too.

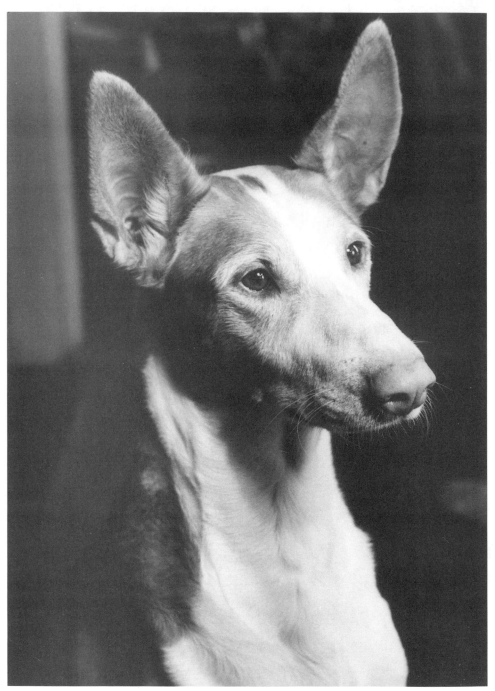

Training is essential for all dogs to enhance the canine-human bond. Done correctly, dog training combines both science and art so that the dog is controllable and predictable but not zombielike or mechanical.

10

Training Your Dog

$\mathbf{D}$OG TRAINING is an art and a science. The art entails patience, self-control and empathy, and the science includes compassionate understanding and a knowledge of some elementary principles of animal behavior and psychology. But only too often, knowledge alone is applied as power and control over the animal. A well-trained dog is not a submissive, obedient zombie, conditioned to gratify its owner's egotistical desire to be "master." I have seen dogs who have been trained with remote-control electro-shock collars. They are indeed obedient, but such inhumane "hi-tech" training is unnecessary and costly, and it does not establish a close rapport between the dog and its owner-trainer, and can turn the dog into a mindless automaton. In the wrong hands, these widely promoted devices also cause unnecessary pain, fear and anxiety.

All you need is love, patience, a six-foot-long leash, a training collar and a twenty-foot-long leash to teach your dog various word-commands. I will shortly describe a basic training procedure for you to follow, but a little background understanding is needed before launching into a training program.

The more dependent your dog is upon you, the easier it will be to train. This is why I advise people to adopt a puppy between six and ten weeks of age, since this is the period when a pup most readily becomes bonded to its owner. The better it is socialized, the more dependent, willing and trainable it will be.

No matter how old a dog is, however, it can be taught new tricks. All dogs are capable of being trained, but not all dog owners are able to train their dogs. Some breeds, like Poodles, Shelties, Golden and Labrador Retrievers and German Shepherds, are much easier to train than others. But even the most difficult breeds and recalcitrant individuals can learn basic commands and become more reliable and enjoyable companions.

If you feel incapable of assuming a dominant, authoritative role over your dog as its "pack-leader," then your chances of making it obey you are very slim. So if you feel that your dog is too much for you to handle even after trying the basic training steps outlined in this chapter, I strongly urge you to sign up for a course at a local dog obedience training school.

All dogs should be controllable and obedient to some degree, for their own good and for the benefit of others. Dogs that run into traffic or challenge their owner's authority by biting or jumping all over visitors are a menace to themselves and society. In sum, all good dogs should have some training. A lack of proper training turns potentially good dogs into bad ones.

Never hit your dog or lose your temper during a training session. Both actions will make your dog either afraid or aggressive, thus making it more difficult to handle and less able or willing to learn. If your dog is making lots of mistakes or seems to be progressing too slowly, back off. Overtraining, pushing your dog and yourself too hard, is the worst thing that you can do. Stop training for a couple of days and then begin slowly, taking your dog through what it already knows.

The three basic principles of training are control, motivation and reward. You must learn to control your dog by getting its attention, first by calling its name, making eye contact with it and having it look directly up at you. Initially, a leash and collar will be needed, which gives you additional control until the dog understands you and has acquired some self-control. Training commands such as "Sit" and "Stay" also teach the dog to be passive and submissive toward you. By praising the dog verbally ("Good Fido, clever dog") in a friendly, approving tone and patting it on the head every time it responds correctly, you are rewarding it for behaving submissively and obediently toward you.

Being obedient and submissive becomes a *pleasurable* experience for the dog if it is taught correctly. This is the best way to prevent your dog from ever becoming aggressive toward you and from challenging your authority. If you do not give effusive praise when the dog comes when called, or sits on command, and instead literally dominate it into compliance by pulling on its choke-chain collar, as many professional trainers do (or worse, use a shock-collar), you will not make learning pleasurable for the dog. The end result could be that you create an overly submissive or shy dog, or one that is a slow learner because it does not enjoy working with you. In sum, too much control and not enough praise will adversely affect a dog's motivation, willingness to learn and eagerness to respond.

After each training session I also advise some extra reward, to further enhance the dog's motivation, such as a good grooming or a long walk around the neighborhood. I do not advise feeding immediately afterward, since some dogs will think about nothing but being fed and will not perform well, and will do even worse when not hungry.

Don't be afraid to discipline your dog for inattention. When appropriate, a harsh "No" should suffice, followed by a quick but not hard jerk on the leash to literally snap the dog to attention. However, too much correction and insufficient praise is the wrong way to go. If you find this happening, either you are pushing your dog too hard and too fast or you should sign up for lessons at a local canine obedience class. Whenever your dog runs off and eventually comes back after ignoring your command to "Come," *never* punish, since it will come to associate coming back to you with punishment. Always reward. Many people unwittingly train their dogs to run off by punishing them when they return. Likewise, if it makes a mistake during training, *don't* punish: simply call it back, get it under control, praise and reassure and start all over again.

DON'T USE A CHOKE CHAIN ON YOUR DOG

Some experienced veterinarians and dog trainers are now seriously questioning the wisdom of using a choke chain on dogs for training. A dog should never wear a choke chain all the time, because it is not uncommon for one front claw to get hooked into it, which can cause panic to the dog and damage to the foot.

For training a dog to heel and not to pull on the leash, a broad leather or nylon collar can be just as effective as a choke chain.

Owners who use choke chains to stop dogs from leash pulling generally give a loud verbal reprimand and then pull hard on the leash, which snaps the chain. This can cause the dog considerable pain and may cause permanent damage to the neck. A far better way is to simply stand still when the dog is pulling ahead and command the dog to "heel" while braking it by maintaining pressure on the leash and moving up alongside and in front of the dog. As soon as the dog has been passed by the owner, it should be rewarded with praise, either with food or with a gentle pat, for being in the position by the owner's heels, which is the desired position to prevent the animal from forging ahead. This kind of training sequence rewards the dog for being close to the owner and is far more effective than giving the animal a painful jerk with the choke chain when it is out in front of the owner.

The pain and trauma caused by the owner's suddenly snapping the choke chain could interfere with the dog's ability to learn. In contrast, a regular leather or wide nylon collar will give a steady pressure around the dog's neck without causing pain or physical injury.

Although many dog trainers advise their clients to use choke chains to stop their dogs from pulling on the leash, more than one experienced trainer has found that as many as 50 percent of their clients' dogs still pull on the leash with or without a choke chain after they have been through routine training with one. One is led to the inevitable conclusion that a choke chain is cruel and unnecessary. Since its function is to literally choke the dog into obedience, it cannot be considered a humane or enlightened training aid. Furthermore, significant injuries can be caused by these choke chains by people who are too rough, are inexperienced or lose their tempers with the dogs. These include rupturing of the windpipe or severe bruising around the larynx; neuromuscular disorders resulting from constriction and tissue damage in the cervical region of the neck; bruising around the base of the ear causing hypersensitivity to touch and a tendency to bite when handled around the head; and epileptic seizures triggered by constriction of the blood supply to the central nervous system.

While some animal trainers follow the path of power, using all kinds of inhumane devices, more enlightened trainers endeavor to use gentleness and understanding at all times and recognize that choke chains not only can cause injury to dogs but also have limited effectiveness as a training device and are closer to an instrument of torture than one of control.

114

Making certain the dog understands what is expected of it and complete consistency in training sessions help assure favorable results, whether your goal is winning obedience trials or simply having an easy-to-live-with companion.

Evelyn M. Shafer

BASIC STEPS

It is easiest to start training your dog on the leash, using such basic commands as "sit" and "stay" to establish your leadership. These commands put the dog into passive, submissive postures that he will soon learn to enjoy, since he gets praised for adopting them. Choose a quiet place for the lessons where the dog will not be easily distracted. A good time is not when the dog is hungry or ready for a walk: better to feed the dog first and have a training session a couple of hours later, or take it for a short walk and then start the session. I like to use the leash method for teaching a dog the six basic commands, walking with the dog at one's side, initially training him to follow or "heel." This method is faster than simply trying to train the dog facing you, secured by a long leash, and coaxing it to respond with tidbits of food, as many novices have tried. The leash method immediately puts you in charge, prevents the dog from running away and insures sufficient psychological control, putting you in the dominant leader role without having to force the dog into extreme submission through sheer physical force.

Step One: "Heel"

With the leash held across your body in front in your right hand, with your left hand holding the leash near the training collar and with the dog on your left side, call your dog by name and command, "Heel." As you step forward, snap the leash briskly to pull the dog close to your side. Always start off with your left foot and walk at a moderate pace. If the dog struggles and fights the leash, praise and reassure him, and repeat the command, saying his name and "Heel." Once he begins to follow close on command, vary your pace, and also turn left and right and in circles. Praise him ("Good Fido, good dog") constantly as he stays by your left heel. Don't keep the leash tight, which will tire you and make him "hard of neck," a puller who will be difficult and less sensitive to control. Allow a little slack, so that you can snap the leash firmly but not hard, whenever he lags behind or pulls ahead of you. Some people snap the leash much too hard and this can injure a dog's neck. As with pulling on the reins to control a horse by the bit in its mouth, the more subtle and well-timed your pulling on the leash is, the more quickly your dog will learn to obey and understand.

Spend about fifteen to twenty minutes on this "heel" lesson every day until the dog has learned to obey. He will have learned

Training classes are offered in many communities and provide many advantages to the dog owner. Two important ones are the opportunity to train under the supervision of a competent professional, and working in a climate where other animals and people are present. In the top photo owners give their dogs the "Stay" signal prior to leaving them on a "Long Sit." In the bottom photo, the dogs have been placed on a "Long Down" and the owners have left the area. All obedience exercises originated from practical considerations based on daily living with dogs. *Jim Abrams*

117

when he stays by your left heel at all times once you give the command "Fido, heel," and when he requires only one or two corrections to stay at heel during the entire training session.

Step Two: "Sit"

Now that he's under control and is used to the leash and training collar, the next important lesson is to learn to sit on command. Call your dog to heel, walk a short distance, then stop and say, "Fido, sit," switching hands so that your right hand is holding the leash near the collar and your left hand is on the dog's rump. Pull up on the leash with your right hand and push down on the dog's rump with the left. Once he is in the "sit" position at your left side, praise him effusively. This makes the submissive posture of sitting pleasurable and rewarding.

Then say his name, call him to heel and walk a few paces before repeating "Fido, sit." After a few days he will have learned to anticipate neck and rump pressure and will sit on command without your having to pull and push him into the sit position. Once he has accomplished this, you can move on to teaching him to stay.

Step Three: "Stay" and "Come"

Call your dog to heel, walk a few paces, put him into "sit" and then say "Stay," raising your right hand over his head and moving around to stand in front of him. Initially he will get up to follow you, so return to his right side, put him into the "sit" position and give the "stay" command: "Fido, stay." If he rolls over submissively, don't play into his behavior. Ignore it, call him to heel and repeat. Eventually he will remain sitting and stay as you move away. Here you may wish to use a longer leash and keep him in "stay" for thirty seconds or more, with your right arm upward and toward you, waving him to come as you say "Fido, come." Once he reaches you, give him lots of praise, then go through heel, sit, stay, and then come once more. A fifteen-minute session every day for one to two weeks should suffice. Then you can start increasing the duration of "stay" to one to two minutes.

Step Four: "Down"

The last command to be learned is "down." Put him in "sit," and then lift his front legs up, sliding them forward so that he goes into a lying position as you say "Fido, down." With one hand pressing down on his shoulders, repeat the words *down* and *stay* four or five times and then *heel* and allow him to get up. After a few days of teaching "down" combined with "stay," you can use the long leash and move around in front of the dog, who is in the "sit" position, keeping one arm up to hold him in "stay." Then lower your arm, saying "down" at the same time. If he mistakes your arm signal for "come," put him back into "sit" and "stay" and repeat until he will go from "sit" and "stay" to "down" when he sees your arm go down and hears you give the command "Fido, down."

Once these four steps are mastered, and your dog has learned the five basic commands—heel, sit, stay, come and down—you can try your dog off the leash. This will take some time and patience, and will involve repeated sessions on the leash until he has learned to respond to voice and arm signals independent of leash control. Then you will have an obedient, reliable and well-mannered dog, who will come when called, stay down when told to instead of jumping on visitors, sit by the roadside on command, and generally be a much better-adjusted companion.

Don't have absolute faith in your powers as a trainer, however. Dogs will break the rules with sufficient temptation and run off with other dogs to court and play, and even run into traffic. Always keep the dog on the leash in public places. It is illegal in many municipalities not to do so.

You may wish to increase your dog's word comprehension, building upon what he has already learned. You can teach him to "stand and stay," to "roll over," "shake hands," "get up," "get down," "fetch" and "speak" once you have developed control and understanding via the four basic steps in training. And you can become even more sophisticated, using whistle calls or hand signals instead of word commands. Once he has learned the verbal signal, precede it by a specific whistle or hand-arm movement, then omit the verbal command. The latter substitution is especially helpful for older dogs that are becoming deaf.

One final tip: your voice inflection is very important. For passive responses like "down" and "stay," let your tone of voice fall as you say the word and draw the word out slowly—"staaay," "doownn." For active responses such as "come" and "fetch," give an upward inflection at the end of the word, or for emphasis, repeat the words *Fido, come-come!* Keep the words short and crisp.

In summary, what this basic obedience training does is establish you as the pack leader, which is the kind of relationship that all dogs need if they are not to become socially maladjusted, canine delinquents—unsatisfactory companions, even for those people who like to overindulge their dogs and give them a free rein at all times. Basic obedience can be commenced as early as twelve to sixteen weeks of age, but intensive training should not be undertaken until the dog is around six months of age. Never forget after a training session to reward the dog with a good grooming, or exercise and free play with a ball, Frisbee, or tug-of-war towel, and always praise the dog royally when he responds to your commands. If it is done in the proper spirit, obedience training brings out the best in our canine companions, and establishes the right relationship between the owner and the animal. It is the best investment any responsible dog owner can make.

POSTSCRIPT: INAPPROPRIATE DISCIPLINE

People too often discipline their dogs (and even their children) inappropriately. For example, I recently saw a woman screaming and beating her dog with the leash. She had lost her temper. I was following her and she was obviously in too much of a hurry even to let her old dog stop to sniff and mark wherever he chose.

Often we aren't aware of how selfish we are being when we impose our will upon others. It probably would have been better if this woman had not taken her dog out at all. Not long ago I witnessed a dog fight in the park. The dog that got the worst of it was severely reprimanded for fighting by her hysterical owner. She should have comforted the dog, regardless of who started the fight. It always takes two. The silly woman was embarrassed by her dog and was probably terrified of losing control in her own life. Her dog was hurt and frightened. The last thing she should have done was to beat the dog and scream in her face. She probably loved her dog, but her fears got in the way. In the middle of her tirade, her dog suddenly had a seizure, a convulsion that was triggered by the dog's nervous system being overloaded and overcharged by the combination of the owner's and another dog's aggression.

The last, bizarre and disturbing example of inappropriate discipline concerns a man who always pulled wildly on his dog's leash and waved his walking stick ferociously in the air whenever his dog saw another dog and barked at it. The man, afraid his dog might get into a fight, was actually inciting his dog to behave aggressively, though he thought he was disciplining it.

People sometimes treat their animals wrongly when they are not aware of their own feelings and motives. This can result in unnecessary cruelty, even at the hands of otherwise loving owners who are too caught up in themselves to be objective and see that what they are doing is inappropriate.

A good watchdog is valued today just as it has been for centuries. If you feel you need the security such a dog can afford, select a watchdog with a good temperament. Remember that dogs are territorial and almost any dog will bark at the door and alert you to a visitor's presence. Some breeds, such as this Bullmastiff, have been bred to be protective, so their senses would be even more acute in matters of security and protection.

11

Developing a Watchdog

$\mathbf{M}$ANY PEOPLE who have dogs value them not just for the companionship they give, but also for the deep sense of security a good watchdog can give.

By watchdog I don't mean one that attacks strangers or barks all the time. A good watchdog is one that alerts its owner to noises immediately outside the house (not a block away or in the apartment below) and to any suspicious human intrusion by barking. Dogs will do this quite naturally, since they are territorial and become alarmed to varying degrees when they feel their home base is being invaded.

Given this natural propensity, dogs can be easily trained to be good watchdogs. Very often, though, people expect their dogs to become watchdogs without any training and make the dog totally confused by giving it ambiguous signals. A common mistake is to verbally reprimand or physically punish a dog when it barks, say, at a dog outside, or at someone knocking at the door. This will quickly deter a young dog from giving warning barks. One should praise the dog for barking, determine why he's barking and then say "OK, good dog, now quiet" if all is clear. A reassuring voice is all that's needed. If you seem calm, the dog will calm down too.

Agitated, nervous dog owners should "cool it" and not panic

Left: Many people find Toy dogs, such as these Yorkshire Terriers, excellent watchdogs. While they are certainly not physically intimidating, Toys are both highly territorial and very vocal. Often these qualities are all that are required in a reliable watchdog in the home.
Photo courtesy HSUS/Frickey's Studio

Below: The familiar Doberman Pinscher is a highly specialized watchdog and a protection dog of great courage and ability. Obedience training is important for a Doberman, as is an owner who is ready to assert needed authority.

when someone is at the door or when the telephone rings, dropping everything and running to answer. This can confuse dogs, make them anxious and more likely to bark or even to bite their owner every time the phone rings, as has happened on more than one occasion.

It can be difficult to get an easygoing, people-loving pup to bark at the right time. You can't push this, since very young pups aren't very territorial. Territorial barking takes a while to develop, some pups not showing much territoriality until they are six months to a year or more of age.

One way to encourage territorial barking is to stand by the door with the dog and bark whenever someone (ideally another dog) passes by. Or, if you don't want to appear so eccentric, have a neighbor or friend come and knock on your door or ring the door bell and bark in response. Many young dogs will mimic their owners and get the message. If they are too easygoing their motivation can be strengthened by having the person outside make a racket at the door and scare the dog by wearing a paper bag with eye-holes over the head. This will make the dog more alert and suspicious of the "bogey man at the door" after a few sessions. The dog must be rewarded verbally and by petting as soon as it barks, and even encouraged by the owner's barking along with it.

For more timid dogs, I recommend general "self-esteem building" by engaging in tug-of-war games with an old towel or rubber chew and tug toy. Letting the dog feel its strength, allowing it to "win" by letting go of the towel or toy and developing its muscles and self-confidence through such play can turn fearful introverts into better-adjusted extroverts. The younger the dog is when you begin, the better.

I have further validation of the significance of "barking together" from personal experience. On several occasions, when visiting friends with dogs, I have been able to win the dog over either by barking when someone came to the door or by looking out the window or toward the door and barking as though someone were invading "our" territory. The dogs have joined in with me and seemed to like the idea that this two-legged visitor would share the job of defending the dog's own territory.

One dog I heard of was most confused when its owner developed a wheezy, bronchial cough. Every time she coughed suddenly, the dog would bark as though giving support to a territorial bark!

All dogs, except Basenjis, make excellent watchdogs—even Toy breeds—since they are all naturally defensive and protective of their home base. The size of dog makes no difference if you want an animal to be a reliable watchdog, a "lookout" as well as a companion.

However, owners of smaller breeds must avoid the temptation to overswaddle them, because dogs that are overdependent and over-protected can become perpetual puppies and useless as watchdogs.

Sometimes the reverse can happen and a dog can become over-protective to the point that strangers are attacked or visitors threatened and made to feel downright unwelcome. This problem is quite common and can be caused by a number of factors.

The first problem category I first met when making a house call on an elderly couple's dog, a routine vaccination. The dog was so territorial that it tried to attack me and when restrained, bit its master. Dogs raised without any obedience training, and overindulged as well, can become holy terrors, top dogs in the house and garden and a menace to all. They are a frequent cause of neighbor complaints for being allowed to bark excessively, because the over-permissive owners are too indulgent to discipline the animal.

The next problem category is that of the naturally protective breed, such as a German Shepherd or Doberman Pinscher. Such breeds need obedience training so that they can be controlled and will not bark excessively when someone is at the door or react aggressively and protectively when they meet strangers. This problem is compounded when the dog picks up on the owner's paranoia or timidity. Some of the most difficult dogs to handle, in my experience, have been those protective breeds that are owned by apprehensive people whose temperament seems to make the dog even more paranoid and protective. Obedience training is the only answer in such cases.

The protective instinct is so strong in some breeds and individual dogs that other problems can arise that owners should be alerted to. A dog on a leash with its owner or on a chain in the yard is often more aggressive and protective and may bite a passerby or visitor. Some dogs are so protective of and watchful over young children in the family that they may injure other children playing with them or adult passersby.

Because this protective instinct is so well developed in some breeds, and because of their trainability, intimidating size and physical strength, many people like the idea of having such a dog attack trained to make it a better protector. This is a mistake. Such dogs in the inexperienced hands of nonprofessional dog handlers are more a liability than an asset. I recall the case of a delivery boy who was severely mauled when the woman in the house called to him to come in, forgetting that their attack-trained dog was in the living room and not in the backyard.

Such dogs need to be obedience trained, not attack trained. Trainers who advertise that they will make your dog an attack-trained protector often use extremely cruel methods to break the dog's spirit and natural inhibition against biting people. I would not wish to live with a potential canine psychopath that had been so abused and psychologically scarred for life.

It can be argued that a watchdog that just barks isn't sufficient security. Certainly the yaps of a small dog won't scare away all intruders, but most it will, since most intruders are on edge and a barking dog draws attention to them and makes them feel exposed and thus more vulnerable. If you want a larger dog with a deeper bark, a medium-sized Terrier or Standard Poodle will suffice. That the bigger the dog, the more protection you have is only partly true. A protective thirty- or forty-pound dog can be very intimidating and can inflict multiple painful bites. Some large breeds, such as the Irish Wolfhound, are very mild dogs and it's only their size that has any protective value.

I once received an irate phone call from a lady who was mugged in her home while her Collie sat by and watched. She was furious that her dog had not come to her rescue. However, further conversation with the woman confirmed what her tone of voice had suggested: she was extremely controlling and very domineering over her dog. The dog was so subordinated to her (she had probably destroyed its self-esteem) that it probably thought that she could take care of herself.

Not all dogs seem always to understand when their owners are in distress, however, and at other times dogs may become confused and intervene protectively, but inappropriately. Dog owners should be alerted to this problem also. In one instance an elderly lady fell down and in the confusion was attacked by her own two dogs. Another dog owner had a lawsuit on his hands when his dog, on the leash, bit a child who came running up to and then past the dog and its owner to catch a ball. The dog misinterpreted this as a threat, as have dogs who have leaped onto the bed and attacked a man to protect their mistress while the two were making love. Jealousy may be an additional motivation.

People who do have very protective watchdogs that could cause injury to others have a social obligation to put up warning signs that they have such a dog on their property. But still, three-year-olds can't read. There is a law case pending now in which a two-year-old wandered into the yard of a very protective dog that was chained to a log. Regardless of the parents' inattention, the dog owners had a social responsibility to make their yard child-proof, since a dog in an open yard is an attraction and a hazard to any young child.

12

New Babies
and Young Children:
Nipping Problems
Before They Start

ONE OF THE MOST serious concerns for many parents is how their dog will accept a new baby. The best way to cope with this concern is to be informed, and I will spell out what problems you may encounter and what you can do to nip them in the bud, before the baby or someone in the family gets nipped or worse.

The last thing that I want to do is to remove all anxiety. Parents must be constantly vigilant and never feel that they are so secure with their dog or with their knowledge that no accidents could happen. Take the recent case of a couple who returned from the hospital with their newborn baby, introduced the baby to their dog, who was curious, friendly and gentle, set the baby in its carrier on the floor of the living room, and went into the kitchen together. The next moment, the dog was with them, indulgently carrying the baby by its head in its large jaws. The baby died soon afterward from brain hemorrhage. The innocent dog had crushed its soft skull.

On the other hand, I don't want to scare prospective parents to

Dogs and babies are a natural, happy combination. When a new baby joins the family, properly introducing the dog and making sure it is not pushed into the background are important points to observe in keeping everyone happy.

the point of getting rid of their dog. Some doctors have been very irresponsible in this regard, advising pregnant mothers as a matter of routine health care to get rid of a puppy because it can harbor parasites (worms) that can infest children. However, any health expert will tell you that infants are at greater risk when they are around humans than when they are around animals, because most human diseases are carried and transmitted only by humans.

This brings us to the first rule of preparing for the arrival of a new baby. Consult your veterinarian, who will run tests and make sure that your pet is healthy and safe before the baby's arrival.

Second, early on in pregnancy I would strongly advise dog-owning expectant parents to sign up for obedience school so the dog will be easier to handle and control by the time the baby is born.

Many pets do sense that something is going on in the home, especially during the last trimester of pregnancy. This sense can make them more anxious and lead to some problems. A mother's apprehension over or preoccupation with pregnancy can affect the pet because the usual routines change and the animal receives less attention. Some dogs withdraw, or become more solicitous, and this can make things worse because they may be punished for being a nuisance. Certainly, a woman in late pregnancy isn't going to engage in the same long walks and rough-and-tumble games with a dog. The husband must take up the slack and give the dog the attention and exercise that it needs and expects.

A pregnant woman can still pet, groom and talk to her canine companion, and given some indulgence, most pets adjust well. The reduced activity of the expectant mother and the increased focusing of attention on her by the husband can make for a very dependent dog, and it becomes very easy for the family dog to feel rejection when a baby is due. This isn't anthropomorphic speculation. Many couples today have raised their dogs to be very dependent, in some ways using them emotionally as child-substitutes. I have had letters from couples who wonder why their dogs have become less affectionate and even become nuisances during pregnancy or following childbirth. One couple kept their dog out of the forthcoming baby's bedroom, which they were decorating. The well-behaved dog chewed on the closed bedroom door one day when they were out. Then when the door was left open, the dog defecated on the floor by the crib, a sure sign that he was disturbed and confused by the change in daily routine and the reduced attention he was receiving. So the third rule is to be sure to put time in with the dog so that it does not feel neglected or rejected.

A few weeks before the baby is due to arrive it is a good idea to buy a doll, swaddle it and pretend to nurse and cuddle it. Let your dog see what is going on and become habituated to your new behavioral repertoire. A tape recording of a baby crying, played occasionally from within the swaddled doll, will also help your dog more easily accommodate the new baby since it will be less alarmed by the novelty of its presence and your focusing of attention on the infant.

When the baby comes home, even more attention must be showered on the animal to allay jealousy. Dogs do experience and express jealousy, what amounts to sibling rivalry, which is more intense with a more dependent dog.

This can be expressed in a variety of ways. Some dogs will become unhousebroken, or covet their toys and become snappy and sulk. Others become excessively solicitous, especially when the baby is being fed or having its diaper changed, or will follow the owner around the house and resent being left alone. When the pet becomes a nuisance in this way, it is only too easy to forget why it is behaving as it does and to punish it. This will make things much worse. More petting, praise and reassurance are called for.

Some dogs will express their anxiety, jealousy and insecurity by eating excessively (just as some people will). Comforting a displaced pooch with extra food is obviously unwise, since an obese pet is an unhealthy pet, and allowing it to eat more isn't going to help its emotional turmoil.

The fourth rule is to help satisfy the dog's curiosity and allay its fears by introducing it to the baby. Hold the baby protectively in your arms and sit down so the dog can come close and look and sniff. Talk in a quiet, calm and reassuring voice. The animal may be alarmed when baby cries, but should quickly habituate to this. I know of some dogs who will immediately come to a parent when the baby is crying as though to tell him or her to hurry up and take care of things. In fact, the cry of a baby is not unlike the distressed yelp-howls of a puppy, and most pets seem to react with understanding.

The sudden, jerky movements of a baby's limbs can sometimes alarm a dog, or become an attractive stimulus for the animal to paw at or bite at playfully. Such reactions should be inhibited by a word of discipline and these reactions are one reason why the fifth rule must always be followed, and this is to *never* leave the baby alone and unsupervised with the animal.

As the baby matures and is able to reach out and grasp things, such as the dog's ears or tail, this rule becomes even more important.

The dog must be protected from the child. Young infants have a tendency to grab and hold very hard and have no understanding that they are causing pain. Any mother with long hair knows this.

Most dogs are extremely understanding, patient and long-suffering with infants, but even with a wholly reliable pet, accidents and tragedy can happen. Often when a dog has had enough contact with a toddler, he will get up and move away. The toddler should be discouraged from crawling or walking after the animal and a safe "off-limits" place should be set aside for the pet where it can rest undisturbed. The place where the animal eats and drinks should also be off-limits and made childproof with either a gate in the doorway or a crate or cage for the dog to eat in. When the dog is being fed, it should be allowed to eat without any interference. Some dogs when they are eating will act more aggressively, and a warning snap could mean an accidental bite. It is natural for a dog to growl protectively over its food when it feels threatened by the presence of a small child or an adult. One ignorant dog owner told me he would discipline his dog if it growled at him while it was eating, and would actually force the food out of its mouth. He asked me if I thought he should teach his six-year-old son to do the same so the dog would "mind." My advice is to let eating dogs alone, and to let sleeping dogs lie.

No matter how much you trust your dog, accidents can happen, because in truth you can't trust your infant to behave. There was a tragic case not long ago in which a dog killed a child in its own living room. The dog was euthanized and an autopsy done to see if it had some brain abnormality. The veterinarian found a broken pencil rammed right down into the dog's inner ear, which must have caused it intense pain.

Pets have also bitten children because the child accidentally touched an infected ear or injured paw. Some dogs are very protective about their own toys, and an infant isn't going to understand what a warning growl or a snap means. Until the child reaches the age of reason, it is prudent to protect the pet from the child.

Other dog reactions that can lead to some misunderstanding and even amusement at times are tied in to the dog's natural instincts. Some dogs will nuzzle into a baby's diapers to clean the baby, just as it would a puppy. Other dogs enjoy rolling in the contents of a discarded diaper. More than one dog has regurgitated food for a human infant, something that all wild canids do to feed their pups at weaning time.

The rule of vigilance also extends to neighbors' children, especially if you have a protective dog playing with them and your own

Growing up with a responsive dog builds character in a child. The love and companionship the dog provides helps develop the qualities of patience and compassion in a youngster. *Photo courtesy HSUS/Eric Friedl*

child or children. One of my consultees had a German Shepherd who was so protective of "her" children that she would stop them from playing too wildly with neighbor children if the latter seemed to be threatening those of her family. Fortunately, this dog was sufficiently aware, rational and understanding that it did not injure or even scare the other children. But other, less intelligent dogs often will frighten, if not injure, others' children. This does not mean the dog is vicious, just that it is too instinctively impulsive and not stable and rational enough to be totally reliable. Most dogs are biologically unreliable. It is part of their nature, as with the gentle dog carrying the baby and crushing its skull, a biological accident that no dog can be held responsible for because its nature is such that it is not totally adapted to domesticated life with humans.

Growing up with a responsive dog provides the child with companionship and security; a sense of being important and loved when greeted by the animal; a sense of empathy when the dog is sick and when the pet responds to the child when the child is sick or unhappy; a sense of competence and heightened self-esteem when a loving dog obeys and submits. And ultimately through such love from another being, a child will come to be humane, compassionate and respectful of all life. But if a child is wholly deprived of all animals, this eventuality is most unlikely.

13

The Four Rs of Dog Rights, Health and Owner Responsibility

W ISDOM'S "FOUR PILLARS" of veterinary preventive medicine and health-care maintenance are as follows: *right understanding, right environment, right breeding,* and *right feeding.* These are the basic rights of all animals under our dominion.

These four principles are complementary and synergistic. A weakness or deficiency in any one of these may be compensated for to some degree by the others. The probability of disease increases in proportion to the degree of weakness or deficiency in any one of these four pillars, and also increases with a lack of synergy or compensatory support between them. For example, without right understanding, the problems of a dog afflicted with an unstable temperament (which could be a product of wrong breeding) can be exacerbated. Likewise, with wrong feeding, the health problems of animals with a genetic predisposition to metabolic or endocrine disorders can be aggravated.

Such are the dynamics of these four interrelated and interde-

136

pendent principles. *Right understanding* entails knowing and satisfying an animal's basic behavioral and emotional requirements. This includes proper socialization and rearing to establish a close emotional bond between the person and the animal, where the animal is neither overindulged, neglected, nor subjected to excessive control or physical or psychological abuse.

Right environment entails providing the animal with conditions conducive to the expression and satisfaction of its basic physical and psychological needs, in such a way that its adaptability to domesticity is not jeopardized. Opportunities for exercise, play and affiliation with other animals (for example, by keeping two dogs instead of one) are all part of providing the right environment for the animal. The animal should also be provided with various toys, an outdoor run or enclosure and a secure sleeping place.

Right breeding entails careful attention to the elimination of the disorders that arise as a result of inbreeding and selection for abnormal traits in purebred dogs. An alternative is to promote the ownership of dogs, mongrel or purebred, with a significantly lower incidence of such anomalies, which can cause unnecessary suffering and increased susceptibility to disease.

Right feeding entails providing animals with a wholesome, balanced diet. This will vary according to the breed, size, temperament and age of the animal, as it does also when the animal is growing, pregnant or convalescent.

Greater emphasis must be placed upon these four principles in the education of veterinary students and in the education of dog owners and breeders. Since these animals provide people with the many benefits of their companionship and unconditional love, we surely owe them no less: right understanding, right environment, right breeding and right feeding. These principles may be regarded as the basic rights of companion animals and their recognition will contribute significantly to the prevention of unnecessary suffering and to their overall well-being.

LEAVE IT TO NATURE?

There is a widespread attitude, if not a superstition, that when an animal is sick, "Nature will take care of things." It is difficult to convince pet owners who believe this that Nature takes care of nothing. Animals in the wild take care of themselves (as by eating medicinal herbs, fasting, withdrawing and resting) and of each other

The dogs around us are purely a product of our own environment, so when they become sick or injured, we cannot allow "nature to take its course." Faced with a dog in need of veterinary attention, we have the responsibility of having the dog treated as soon as humanly possible. *Evelyn M. Shafer*

(sick or injured wolves are often fed, groomed and protected by packmates).

To let "Nature" care for sick or injured pets is the height of irresponsibility. The house pet is neither natural nor a part of Nature.

"Leaving it to Nature" can also be a kind of denial. People don't want to have to worry about a sick pet, so it's more comfortable, if not convenient, to let a sick animal alone.

While veterinarians don't agree with all my views, they are unanimous in their agreement that the leave-it-to-Nature attitude is a widespread problem in the pet-keeping public. No, they aren't simply rooting for more business. They do recognize that animals have rights, or at least one right, and that is to receive proper veterinary attention when they are sick or injured.

COAT AND SKIN CARE: BEAUTY AND THE BEAST

Not too long ago I saw a beautiful coyote loping across the desert out West in the Sierras. It was early morning and the low light shone off the animal's lustrous coat as though the coyote had been wrought of burnished bronze and gold. Wild animals do radiate health and vitality, and indeed it is the quality of the animal's fur or "pelage" that clearly reflects its overall physical well-being. This may be one of the reasons people like to have their pet's pelage looking neat and lustrous. No one enjoys looking at a disheveled, unkempt animal, or person for that matter. Outward appearances do give an indication of inner physical and also psychological well-being. As a sick dog will not groom itself and will quickly become an unesthetic, pathetic-looking creature with no "bloom" to its coat, likewise a depressed person will often have little interest in his or her personal appearance. We all know, at least unconsciously, that our own outward appearance affects not only how others feel toward us but also how we feel about ourselves. Well-groomed and neatly turned out, we get the attention and affirmation of others, and our self-esteem and self-confidence rise, and likewise when we dress up our children and people compliment us on their appearance. So too, when we do a fine job grooming our dog and trimming it as needed, people notice and we get complimented. Our self-esteem rises. We also enjoy the presence of an attractive animal bubbling over, at least on the surface, with health and vitality.

But does looking good do anything for the pet's sense of self-esteem or overall well-being? Some people have told me vehemently that a good grooming or thorough "beauty treatment" does wonders for a dog's self-esteem. Others say that that's all anthropomorphic nonsense, and that animals are incapable of having such human feelings. So who's right?

Making your dog look beautiful will make it feel good, and I will prove that in a moment, with some clear and concrete scientific evidence. Whether a good grooming or beauty treatment improves your dog's self-esteem or self-image is something else. I, for one, do not doubt that animals have a sense of self, but grooming per se will not, I believe, give a boost to your pet's ego. Being complimented on having a beautiful pet brimming over with vitality is certainly a boost to the owner's ego. And I am convinced that a pet that does look beautiful enjoys the extra attention that its good looks evoke from people. This isn't being anthropomorphic.

Look at some of the top-winning show dogs, simply radiant in the ring and loving every moment of attention they get from human admirers. It probably matters little between dogs whether they are looking good—how they smell is probably just as or even more important than how they look. But living in a humanized world as domesticated animals, dogs do learn that when they are looking good they receive more human attention. Few can resist touching a freshly groomed and puffed-out Poodle, and many will watch with sheer joy as a neatly tonsured Schnauzer or silky-coated, gleaming Irish Setter walks by with owner on the leash. And many a dog frequently becomes more alert and responsive when a passerby stops to say, "What a fine-looking dog you have there."

The scientific evidence for the beneficial effects of grooming, I have described in detail in my book entitled *The Healing Touch*. Briefly, grooming, like massage, stimulates the circulation and the hair follicles of the skin, helping remove loose and dead hair and scales of skin (which are shed and replaced cyclically). Grooming adds sheen to the coat by releasing and spreading natural oils from the oil glands in the hair follicles or "roots." Since grooming stimulates the blood and lymphatic circulations, as does massage, it will be extremely beneficial for aged and convalescent animals. Such stimulation may not only be invigorating, it may also promote the growth of a luxuriant coat. The act of grooming, like that of petting, results in very deep relaxation and a dramatic slowing of the dog's heart rate rhythm, which, as I describe in my massage book, is not only a pleasurable sensation for the animal, it will also help a young or sick animal digest food better and will certainly help animals cope better with and even overcome certain physical and emotional

The down side: This typical American pariah dog represents the millions of unwanted animals in our society today. Homeless and neglected, they cannot fend for themselves in our highly mechanized society, but they can and do reproduce faster than we can control their numbers. *Photo courtesy HSUS*

The up side: This champion Tibetan Terrier reflects the ultimate in breeding, training and care. This beautiful animal represents a large commitment to the dog's physical and emotional needs. Would that this lucky dog's lot could extend to all others. *John L. Ashbey*

stresses and sickness in general. My two dogs come running when they see me with their brushes, ready to give them a thorough grooming, a clear sign of how much they enjoy it.

Skeptics might say pets don't need beauty treatment since, after all, their counterparts in the wild don't have anyone to groom them and keep them looking in top condition. However, in the wild, the animals and living conditions are completely different from our environment. We keep pets that are genetically very different from wild animals, and wild animals don't need any help in keeping healthy and looking good. Having to actively hunt every day keeps wild dogs supple and trim, and as they are in harmony with the seasons, their coats are thick and lustrous in the winter and light and airy in the summer. Keeping our pets indoors can disrupt the seasonal cycles of coat shedding and regrowth, so that some dogs have a thick coat in the summer or a sparse coat in winter. And we have changed dogs genetically, so that some have unnaturally long coats, never shed or have thick underfur year round. Thus as a consequence of indoor living and genetic changes, most dogs need some help in keeping their coats in good condition. Also they do not hunt and eat their own natural foods, but instead enjoy an easy life of being given processed commercial dog foods and table scraps. Diet will influence how well your dog looks, and nutrition certainly affects how lustrous its coat is. More of this later. There are some additional advantages to consider from giving your dog a daily grooming and a beauty treatment (which I will detail shortly) every few weeks. Many dogs have a very strong "doggy" odor and a thorough grooming and beauty treatment will help control this. Even though you may get used to this odor, which comes especially from the dog's skin and ears, visitors may well find it obnoxious.

Dogs with long coats that tangle easily require daily grooming, otherwise tangled balls of hair will quickly develop beneath the ears, on the "feathers" or long hair on the legs, especially between the hind legs, and along the tail and belly. In veterinary practice I had on many occasions to anesthetize animals in order to remove large mats and balls of hair, which can cause considerable discomfort, stop the skin from being properly aerated and lead to skin infections beneath the mats. Owners complained that their pets would not tolerate being groomed, or that it was too much trouble. However, having to tranquilize or anesthetize a dog every time it has to be thoroughly groomed is a health risk. Repeated treatments can result in liver damage and increasing intolerance to anesthesia. But there is nothing else to do if an animal is frightened or acts aggressively when you

142

try to groom it, snip away mats and trim its feathers. The solution is simple: start out right from the beginning with a pup, especially with a long-haired variety, and teach it to accept regular grooming. The earlier in life puppies get used to being groomed and handled, the more willing they will be to be groomed and the easier they will be to handle later in life. Dogs often like to lie over on one side to be groomed so don't insist that your dog sit up or stand. Work on one side and then just grab hold of the dog's front and hind legs and roll it on the other side, repeating the process.

During grooming, you will be able to feel and see any abnormalities, such as a swelling or a red or scaly area of skin that may require veterinary treatment. Owners who groom their pets regularly are more likely to spot when their dog may have something wrong with it. When a problem is identified early, veterinary treatment is often more effective than if a problem has been allowed to develop unnoticed for weeks. This could mean the difference between life and death.

Some groomers like a variety of different combs and brushes. I prefer a two-sided brush, one of stiff bristle and the other of wire embedded in rubber. To begin grooming, I call the animal, get it settled and then stroke it reassuringly around the head. I run my fingers down the animal's back quite hard, several times, to loosen any dead hair, and then push my fingers into the pile of the coat and work upward from the animal's tail to its head.

If the atmosphere is very dry and "staticky," especially in winter, I moisten my fingers (and the brush) first and only groom the animal on a wool rug or cotton towel, in order to reduce the chance of my giving the animal a painful electrical shock. Vigorous brushing and this finger stroking grooming-massage, especially with the animal on a nylon carpet in winter, will charge the animal up and give it repeated electrical shocks.

After loosening the fur with the fingers, I groom the dog in slow, deep, long strokes from head to tail. If the animal is shedding a lot, I make short strokes as I work down the back, removing the hair as needed from between the bristles of the brush. For long-haired dogs, I twist the brush outward, away from the body, as I brush through the coat, also along the tail, so as to fluff out the hair and stop it from getting tangled. I moisten the brush slightly if the fur gets "staticky," because it is more likely to get snarled then.

Long, tangled feathers are best loosened with fingers and comb: a strong stainless steel comb is ideal. Don't use the wire brush side near your dog's face: you could easily poke him in the eye. I always

All dogs require grooming, just as all people do. Naturally, profusely coated animals like this Old English Sheepdog will need more attention than a German Shepherd or a Beagle. In selecting a dog, know in advance how much grooming you are willing to do. *Evelyn M. Shafer*

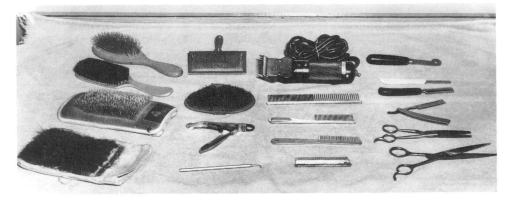

Dog grooming tools are available in an almost infinite variety. The tools you need will depend on the kind of coat your dog has and the kind of grooming you plan to do. A brush and comb, a toenail clipper and a tooth scaler are essential for every dog. *Evelyn M. Shafer*

finish with the bristle side of the brush around the face and then briskly brush down the back with the bristle side to give the coat a final sheen.

Always apologize if you accidentally knock some bony protuberance such as a knee or shoulder with the edge of the brush and give the animal a reassuring stroke as well. Aggregations of hair on the floor after you finish can be vacuumed up or if very clingy with static, wiped up easily with a moist sponge.

When dogs are "blowing" their coats—that is, are shedding the thick pile or undercoat that provides them with so much insulation for the winter—you should not keep raking hard with the wire side of the brush, as that will make your dog's skin hypersensitive. Don't brush hard those areas that have not yet loosened up either. You may well find that your dog has a very clear molting pattern, the hair first loosening around the legs and thighs and then working gradually up the back. So work on these areas and wait for the "shed to spread." I either pluck out the loose pile of underfur as it begins to lift or twist it out with a steel comb. With dogs that have long guard hairs that lie over the undercoat, which are usually shed later, the long hairs tangle very easily with the undercoat. Such tangles are best loosened with fingers or a steel comb: if they are very matted, scissors will be needed to trim out the mats.

Some people inadvertently bathe the dog before stripping out the dead underfur. While, admittedly, soaking the coat helps loosen the underfur, the coat is more likely to tangle when it is wet, so I do not advise bathing before grooming a dog whose coat is "slipping" or shedding.

How often should you bathe your pet? This is part of its regular beauty treatment, and need be done only when the doggy odor is strong and the coat excessively oily, as in Terriers and related breeds and some mixed breeds. Excessive bathing is to be avoided, since it will remove too many of the natural oils that help keep the coat in condition and will result in a dry, lackluster pelt. Also, bathing too often can disturb the delicate balance of natural bacteria that live on the skin, and when this balance is disturbed, skin infections are more likely to develop. Dogs that live outdoors should rarely be bathed (you will want to bathe them when they roll in manure or get hit by a skunk, in which case cover the animal in ketchup or tomato sauce for a while to absorb the skunk's scent), because the oils in the skin provide protection from rain and cold.

The more the dog struggles while being bathed, the more difficult the job is and the more likely it is that the dog will hate having a bath the next time. It's difficult to make the bath a pleasant experience, as it is for a child with a rubber duck and other toys to play with in the bath. Talk to your dog in a reassuring voice and be sure to have a rubber mat in the sink or bath so the animal won't slide around when its feet are wet and it starts to panic. Never dip the dog into the water. It's best to calm the animal first and then wet it slowly all over with a sponge. Rub the shampoo in well and let it "sit" for a few minutes before thoroughly rinsing. Soapy suds tend to build up on the animal's underparts, which will need additional rinsing.

I use a mild shampoo to bathe my dogs, first sponging the dog over with warm water, then rubbing in the shampoo, which can be hosed off with warm water outside or rinsed off with the animal standing in a sink or bath indoors. To avoid getting soap and water in the ears, you may wish to place a ball of cotton in each ear canal. A little Vaseline around the dog's eyes will help keep shampoo out of its eyes, especially in shaggy breeds whose faces are covered with hair.

With dogs with skin folds, like wrinkled Bulldogs and Bloodhounds, be sure to shampoo well and dry thoroughly, since such folds are a constant potential source of skin trouble. For dogs with minor skin problems and those that cross paths with the occasional flea, a soaking in lemon shampoo is soothing and also helps repel fleas and biting insects in the summer. Remove the rind from one lemon, chop up the rind and let soak overnight in a gallon of just-boiled water. Put this lemon shampoo on your dog after it has had its regular shampoo and allow to seep into the coat for fifteen minutes before drying with a towel or hair dryer. Repeat at weekly intervals to repel fleas.

Ears can be cleaned with warm olive oil or baby oil, removing excess with cotton swabs. First pull out any hair that may be matting the ear canals, which is a common problem in certain heavy-coated breeds. For very dirty and smelly ears (a common source of a strong doggy odor), get a cerumenolytic ear cleaner, which will break down the ear wax and debris, from your veterinarian.

As an alternative you can give your dog a dry bath with talcum powder rubbed into the coat. Let the talcum stay in the coat for ten to fifteen minutes before brushing out. This is an excellent way of removing excess oils and doggy odor. Don't forget to talc between the toes, since the feet especially can produce a strong odor.

It is a good idea to pull or trim some of the long "feathers" from between your dog's toes, since these can get matted and cause irritation and interdigital skin problems. You may also wish to trim some

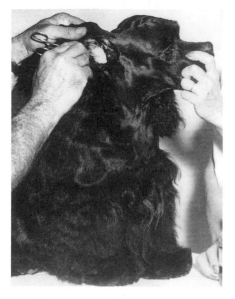

Left: Every dog's ears should be checked periodically and gently cleaned as required. Ear infections can be a persistent problem and if your dog shows the symptoms, your veterinarian should be consulted quickly.
Evelyn M. Shafer

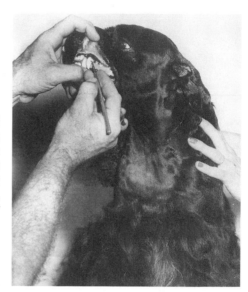

Right: Just as with humans, a buildup of plaque on a dog's teeth soon results in a hard layer of tartar. Ask your veterinarian about your dog's oral hygiene and what you can do to avoid the problems that come from neglected teeth.
Evelyn M. Shafer

Below: This Afghan Hound is being blow-dried following a bath. How often a dog is bathed depends on the individual coat, body chemistry and requirements of dog and owner.
Evelyn M. Shafer

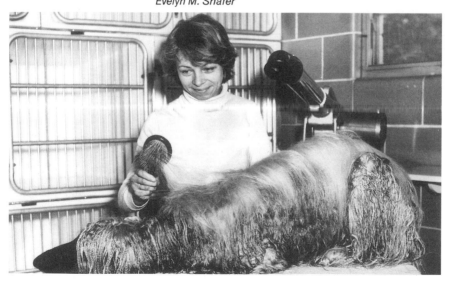

of the feathers of long hair from under the chin, under the chest and down the legs. I do this with my own dog Benji, to stop him from getting soaked and tangled in the winter and from getting ice balls between his toes. Also, remember to wash your dog's feet if it has been out on a salted street in the winter, otherwise the salt may make his paws raw and painful. Removing excess feathers also helps in the summer to stop humid hot spots or skin inflammation from developing and reduces the chances of the hair matting with grass awns, some kinds of which can actually penetrate the skin and cause considerable irritation. Very heavy-coated dogs should be clipped or stripped to make life easier for them in the summer.

After the shampoo, coat trimming and ear cleaning, the final touches of the beauty treatment, before you give your dog a brisk grooming to smooth out and shine up the coat, is to clean the eyes and trim the toenails. Do not use plain water to clean the eyes: use weak boric acid solution or human eye drops. With dogs that have long hair over their faces, be sure to trim or tie back long hair that may be causing chronic eye irritation. No breed, Old English Sheepdogs included, should be left with long hair hanging over their eyes so they can't see, no matter how cute it may look. It's just asking for eye problems and hypersensitivity to light if the eyes are covered all the time.

Toenails are best trimmed with special nail clippers that you can purchase, along with brushes, combs and shampoo, from your local pet store. Dogs that spend much time indoors, whose nails don't wear down sufficiently, frequently need their nails clipped. Also check the thumb or dewclaw nail since these, if untrimmed, will sometimes grow right back into the pad and cause pain and lameness. Snip the nails so that they just touch the ground when your dog has its paw placed squarely on the ground. Avoid snipping too close to the pink quick (invisible in dogs with black nails) since if you cut the quick accidentally you will cause pain and bleeding. A touch of coagulant or simply pressure with a fingertip for a few minutes will usually soon stop any bleeding.

Finally, check your dog's teeth—they may need cleaning to remove tartar buildup. If you see brown scale on the back teeth, a trip to the vet is in order. You can stimulate gums and clean the teeth by wrapping a cotton gauze strip or bandage around one or two fingers and rubbing it around the dog's teeth and gums. Some breeds, especially Toy breeds, need daily dental hygiene. That's a different matter, not part of the regular beauty treatment, and is a problem in part created by breeding for such small size and, in some cases, short muzzles.

Poor diet certainly influences the quality of an animal's pelage and its overall appearance. If your dog has a dry, lackluster coat, it probably needs more vegetable oil in its food, such as linseed, sunflower or safflower. Give one tablespoon per thirty pounds body weight daily and once the coat looks good, reduce that to one teaspoon per thirty pounds body weight. Dry pet foods tend to be low in polyunsaturated fats and high in carbohydrates, so in addition to giving vegetable oil to boost the fat in the diet, try also feeding a high-protein, moist canned food. The addition of a few drops of Vitamins A, D and E, and a pinch of powdered kelp (seaweed) and brewer's or nutritional yeast (working up to a half teaspoon per thirty pounds body weight daily) is a kind of internal beauty treatment that will pay dividends. A chronically poor-looking coat needs veterinary attention, since diet alone won't rectify a hormonal imbalance or worm infestation, two of a number of factors that may make an animal look rundown.

Cutting a dog's hair is sometimes necessary for the animal's well-being. Sometimes it isn't. Owners are often confused over this, which at first sniff seems like a trivial issue. For the dog, though, it often isn't.

An example was the owner who wrote to me for advice over suing her vet, who had given her pet a patchy haircut. The animal had "holes" in its coat and was so unsightly, the woman was embarrassed to have anyone see her pet until the hair had grown back. But the animal was suffering from a mild skin infection and the owner thought the problem could have been cured with an injection and some ointment rubbed into the affected areas.

However, it is bad practice not to remove the hair over quite a large area to stop skin infections from spreading.* Furthermore, the hair that lies over a "hot spot" or other skin disorder provides the ideal breeding ground for bacteria, especially secondary staph infections, which produce smelly pus and will delay the healing of wounds, sores, hot spots and other skin maladies. So the more hair is removed, the better and sooner the skin will heal.

---

*Animals should be discouraged from licking sores only if they are doing so excessively and delaying the healing process, because saliva contains its own healing agents, which normally accelerate wound repair and recovery from infection.

It is advisable to trim the "feathers"—the long hair on the hindlegs of long-haired dogs, especially those that are overweight and cannot clean themselves easily. This will prevent the hair from matting into clumps, which can cause some discomfort. If these clumps get soaked in urine, they can be a source of infection as well as unpleasant odor. It is surprising how many people will let an animal suffer for quasi-esthetic reasons, rather than getting the scissors out and giving it a good trim—or letting a groomer do the job.

SYNOPSIS: BENEFITS OF REGULAR GROOMING

A regular grooming and attention to the animal's coat and skin is part of the responsible custodianship of our four-legged companions. Indeed it is one of their "rights," and the benefits are many. I documented in my book on massage therapy, entitled *The Healing Touch,* that the social activity of grooming has a bonding function, as between mates and parents and offspring. And grooming causes a marked decrease in heart rate, part of the "relaxation response."

Social animals, such as dogs, often groom each other regularly, so it is quite natural for companion animals to enjoy being properly and regularly brushed and combed and occasionally bathed. It *is* unnatural, especially for a dog deprived of the companionship of its own kind, never to be groomed by its human companions. This is one of the reasons two dogs living in the same house are often happier and healthier than those who live just with humans.

Grooming, more so than occasional petting, will evoke the physiologically beneficial relaxation response. This will not only bond your animal companion closer to you, it is also a wonderful way of communicating and of expressing devotion—a kind of communion, if you wish. The beneficial physiological and emotional stimulation grooming provides will also improve the animal's health and immune system because the relaxation response helps rest the overworked adrenal-gland stress-response system. Many often overweight and lethargic dogs are understressed. For them, a vigorous grooming is a "pick-up," and is wisely followed by games, outdoor exercise and any activities that will rouse the animal to play and explore.

Their environment (especially artificial heat and light) disturbs their natural, seasonal coat-shedding and hair growth cycles and can even affect the pigment of the hairs in some animals. Thus many indoor dogs need constant grooming, because they are shedding and growing hair constantly.

Genetically altered coats, ranging widely as they do from the long and tangling to the fluffy, never-shedding and always-growing varieties, need special attention, and often professional help. Many dog breeds could never exist in the wild for long with the kinds of coats that we have given them. This makes it even more our responsibility, and our moral duty, to care for their coats and grooming needs. It is a cruelty of neglect to not properly provide for an animal's grooming requirements.

Genetically altered (for example, long-backed) animals and the obese, aged, arthritic and chronically sick ones who cannot groom themselves properly also need special attention and more frequent bathing.

14

For Better or Worse— How We Affect Our Dogs

I CAN FEEL THE RAGE and frustration rising inside me as I think of a case I once treated. It was a nine-year-old female mutt, a very gentle and intelligent creature that was brought to me because of her sudden and unpredictable "aggressive" behavior. When she growled and sometimes snapped at—but never ever bit—her master, she was severely punished. Such discipline didn't seem to help.

I examined the dog and within moments I found the problem. She had a painfully inflamed and chronically infected ear (caused, I later discovered, by a penetrating barley awn). And she had been punished for being afraid of being petted, even touched near her head.

This true story shows us how we often, usually less severely than in this instance, affect our pets adversely. The causes and consequences are worth reflecting upon because in recognizing them, we can learn to stop ourselves and others from affecting our pets for the worse, and from being cruel and inhumane.

In this instance we can identify ignorance. The master, for no logical reason, assumed that a psychological or mental problem, rather than a physical one, made the dog react as she did. He no doubt felt hurt and rejected when the dog growled or snapped at him and this sense of separation and loss of control led the man to act in anger, striking or kicking the dog. Disciplining the dog automatically for "misbehavior" is a rigid reaction when there is no real thought given as to why the animal is reacting as it is. Anxiety often makes us leap for the controls without any forethought.

With more forethought and understanding, the man would have quickly discovered why his dog was terrified of being touched near its ear. The animal's terror triggered the master's anxiety and sense of vulnerability and of losing control. I know of some animal trainers who have severely maimed and even killed fellow creatures for "being disobedient."

Punishing a dog (by swatting it and rubbing its nose in its own urine) for becoming unhousebroken is as common as the condition is. But usually there is no crime to be punished—animals are rarely deliberately disobedient. Most often the cause is physical, such as a bladder infection or kidney disease, partial blockage or some significant emotional factor (such as the addition of a baby or new pet to the house). How wrong to punish such animals!

Many dog owners punish their dogs for urinating at their feet when they are petting the dog or being greeted by it. Such urination is a puppyish display of subordination, indeed obeisance to the master, who is a leader-parent figure: a god in the dog's eyes, perhaps, but a god who punishes and does not understand and have compassion.

Of course, to be all loving and never give any discipline to your dog affects the animal as adversely as inappropriate discipline. An animal that feels it can always have its own way and has no respect for people is akin to a socially maladjusted, spoiled brat. Appropriate discipline is essential. Too many people either discipline the pet (or the child) inappropriately and inconsistently or are too controlling. Self-control and understanding are prerequisites for good parenting and pet-owning. Lack of understanding can lead to much unnecessary animal suffering. For instance, older dogs with failing kidneys or with diabetes need to drink more water and so need to urinate more often. If they aren't taken outdoors more frequently, they will urinate in the house out of desperation. Ignorant owners will punish the animal or cut down on its water intake, which is cruel and unnecessary treatment.

I consulted with one couple who had a Dachshund, the wife claiming the dog was in pain and had to be carried upstairs and lifted onto the sofa while the husband claimed the dog was spoiled, lazy and just manipulating them for attention. He was probably jealous of the dog. As it turned out, the dog had a slipped disk and needed veterinary attention.

Jealousy toward the pet because it is being given more attention by one spouse is a not uncommon problem. The jealous spouse may then mistreat the poor animal caught up in a family "triangle." People will use pets to keep others at an emotional distance. One man wanted to kill their dog because every time he tried to get close with his wife, the dog would get between them and the wife would ignore the husband's overtures and pet the pooch instead!

Some people are frustrated when their dogs jump up, bark and excitedly prance around in circles or parade around with some favorite toy. Actually the dogs are soliciting attention and greeting their owners. An understanding of pets' behavior, needs and intentions can do much to reduce one's frustration to amusement and acceptance of the animal's spontaneous nature.

Some instances of mistreatment necessitate contacting the local humane society to investigate. A woman wrote to me recently about her neighbor who comes home and screams at her dog and beats it unmercifully, calling it spiteful for having chewed up something in the house or invaded the garbage. Rigorous exercise and games, like playing ball, chasing a stick or a tug of war with an old towel, first thing in the morning and as soon as she came home in the evening, could help her dog vent his spleen and be less bored during the day when he is left alone. A companion cat or leaving a radio on can also help in such cases. Frustration, rage and misinterpreting the animal's behavior in human terms (anthropomorphizing) underlie much animal abuse. The woman's dog wasn't being spiteful. It was being bored to death.

The dog was a Border Collie, a very active, sensitive and highly intelligent animal most unsuited as a breed to a sedentary life and long periods of solitary confinement indoors. The woman eventually found the dog a more suitable home, where its basic needs and breed idiosyncrasies could be better satisfied.

The many breeds of working and "sporting" dogs that man has

Dachshunds are subject to spinal problems due to their body shape. In some cases disease is the culprit, and at other times an injury triggers an episode. Sudden inactivity on the part of such a dog should be investigated to determine whether or not the cause is physical.

The Border Collie was never meant to be a lapdog. This is an active dog with an equally active mind. He belongs where he can keep busy to remain happy.

created with godlike perfection over the centuries demonstrate how creatively we can work with Nature's potential: and more specifically, with the genetic expression of "dogness." The spiritual expression of the dog is in its "dogness"—its freedom to be itself. The joy that a Border Collie expresses from ears and eyes to the tip of its tail when herding sheep is evidence enough that we can create a breed that enjoys the "work" that it has been designed to do. It is inhumane to try to make apartment pets out of Border Collies. They need to be active and want to work. They are so willing, bred to be so highly motivated to work, that they will harm themselves if not treated with understanding. They will chase a Frisbee or other dogs until they drop from exhaustion, which in the summer could mean fatal heat stroke, if they aren't controlled.

But how much control is needed? Too much discipline and inhibition can make some breeds excessively shy while others seem to need more control. It is difficult to know how much control is needed. Here one must know the nature of the breed one is dealing with and learn from others the best way to raise a particular kind of puppy. As a general rule, excessive discipline, never letting the pup "do its thing" and be free to act spontaneously and have its needs gratified, is as bad as over-indulgence—always allowing the animal to have its own way.

We can often learn how best to treat a certain pup by observing how pups of the same breed play together—how active, gentle or rough they are with each other, and what kinds of games they play. And by looking closely at the temperament of the pup's parents, one can grasp intuitively if the pup will grow up to have a boisterous, sedate, timid, gentle, passive, active, aggressive or protective personality (provided the parents have been raised properly).

Too often people choose the wrong temperament for their lifestyles and wants. An active Alaskan Malamute or Border Collie is the wrong dog for a sedentary apartment life, and for someone who wants a cuddly and affectionate dog, a Basenji is the wrong choice. If you want your dog to stay in the yard or not roam far from home, one of the sporting breeds is your worst choice. If you want a graceful-looking dog, don't get an Afghan Hound if you are not prepared to groom it frequently and exercise it for long periods. If you want a purebred dog, my advice is to read all the books you can on the various breeds, visit breeding kennels and dog shows and talk to the dogs' owners and handlers. Finding the right breed for your needs and expectations will help prevent many unfortunate mismatches,

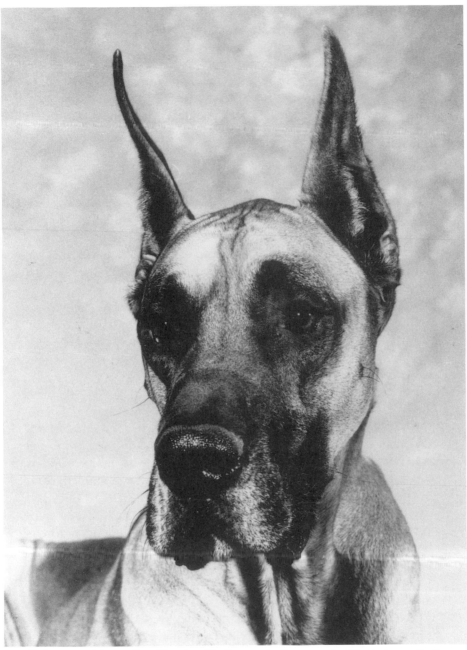

Before acquiring a dog, it's wisest to know what you want and what you don't want. In the face of the tremendous variety (both physical and temperamental) in dogs, advance planning to get the right pet gets you off to the best start. If you don't like grooming, don't get a hairy dog, and if you live in a small apartment, don't get a giant like this fellow. *Photo courtesy HSUS/Botnovcan*

reduce animal (and human) suffering and reduce the numbers of pets being euthanized or abandoned because they are too much trouble or "don't work out."

The creation of dogs is a continuous process, beginning with the basic stock of the many pure breeds that our forefathers evolved for various purposes and continuing with the way in which the pups of these breeds are raised. The more people know about the breed's temperament and basic needs, the better will they be able to find the right breed—or a mixed breed—most suited to their life-style and desires.

Not accepting the temperament or personality of one's pet can also cause the animal unnecessary suffering. It irks me when people ridicule and even punish their pets for being shy or fearful. Verbal abuse, by one's tone of voice, can be rejecting and punitive to a sensitive animal. Recently I met a woman out walking her dog. On seeing my large female dog, her dog put her tail down, whined apprehensively and skittered past us clearly terrified. Her owner chastised her, calling the dog a "stupid chicken." There was no humor or understanding in her voice. The tone was derisive and punitive.

That the dog that one has doesn't have the kind of temperament that one would like is no reason to mistreat it, verbally or physically. But in my experience this is all too common.

It is also important to know how animals communicate with us and what their signals mean. Then they can better understand our communication and intentions. Animals can be harmed, confused and even punished when there is miscommunication and misunderstanding. A father shouting at his son, like a married couple having a verbal conflagration, often make the poor dog in the house feel scared, punished and insecure. Family distress does affect pets emotionally and sometimes physically, sometimes producing such psychosomatic problems as diarrhea, skin problems, self-mutilation, epileptic seizures and asthmatic attacks.

One recent extreme example of miscommunication involved a woman who had just returned from her husband's funeral. She hugged her friend's dog around its neck, probably too intensely because of her grief. The dog felt threatened and bit her seriously in the face. Both the woman's behavior and the dog's were understandable and the consequences unfortunate for both, for the owner had his dog euthanized.

Being more attentive to how we affect our pets emotionally and socially, how we raise them and treat them, can make the difference

158

between a satisfying relationship and one that causes both owners and animals unnecessary stress and distress. For better or worse, we bring animals into our lives, and knowing how to enhance the human-animal bond with love *and* understanding can help bring out the best for man and dog alike.

As we develop a better understanding of the animals with which we share our world, we learn more about how their particular kinds of intelligence, instinct and reasoning power affect their actions. Science has determined that animals do, indeed, have cognitive power and deserve better treatment as fellow beings in an enlightened world.

Missy Yuhl

160

15

Conclusions:
Animal Awareness
and Animal Rights

HOW OFTEN have I heard people pontificate that since animals can't talk, they obviously can't think or reason. The belief that animals act automatically, their minds and actions being controlled by reflexlike instincts, is widespread.

Such thinking may be derived from the old Cartesian philosophy that holds that animals are unfeeling machines. Instincts are seen as fixed programs that control and regulate the animal's life, much as a program fed into a computer "brain" controls the workings of some industrial machinery.

While parts of our brains do function like a complex computer, we can "program" ourselves. We can be rational, objective, change our minds, develop new programs on the basis of experience (learning) and so on. We have insight, reasoning and intuition, above and beyond the hard logic of computer functions. But to accept that some animals also possess such faculties is heresy in many circles. A common retort to such claims is that one is being an-thropomorphic—making animals into "little people" and projecting onto them human attributes that they can't possibly possess because they are *only animals,* and animal means irrational, instinct-controlled automaton. Some take this one step further and suggest that they can't be intelligent because they not only have no language, they don't even have immortal souls like humans.

Blind faith in such enculturated ways of thinking prevents people from really seeing, understanding and appreciating the nature of animals. They cannot understand that instinct is the wisdom of nature genetically encoded in the animal. Instinct is something to stand in awe and wonderment of, not something to demean as subhuman. We, as animals, perform many instinctual actions, such as the nursing movements of a baby and infantile "babbling," smiling and grimacing. Sometimes we can consciously control such instincts, and being able to do so is a sign of maturity and of intelligent self-awareness. We can mimic the facial expression of others because we have not only awareness of others, but also the ability to mimic. Animals, too, have self-awareness and awareness of others to varying degrees, sometimes to a degree exceeding our own (such as a cat or rat's sensitivity to familiar and strange odors). A number of animals have the capacity to mimic and often an understanding of the appropriateness of what they are doing, like the parrot who says "hello" only when people enter the room and "goodbye" only when they leave, and the dog who mimics a human grin only when he is greeting humans. This cannot be put down as simply mechanical conditioning. While conditioning is involved in such learning, there is also clear evidence of awareness in the appropriateness of the various responses in relation to the subtleties of different social contexts.

People may demean animals and deny that they are intelligent and sentient (able to feel pain and to suffer) in order to safely distance themselves from animals. Then, through such rationalizations and defense mechanisms, they become immune from feeling responsible or guilty about how they (and society) abuse animals. Distance (and scientific objectivity) can sever empathy and responsible compassion. People don't like to suffer through empathy with the suffering of animals. Animal suffering (in needlessly repetitive research studies, in testing cosmetics and other nonessential consumer items, in the live trapping of wild animals for their fur, in the atrocious overcrowding of animals on intensive "factory" farms—the list is endless) is justified on utilitarian or economic grounds and rationalized on the basis that animals can't think, aren't intelligent or really aware, and don't really suffer, for when they are hurt, the pain response is just a reflex.

Concrete and irrefutable evidence from sound behavioral, psychological and physiological studies of animals gives us a very different picture. Many species of animals are intelligent, often rational, sensitive, ethical and altruistic. Being so, why should they not be incorporated into the sphere of moral concern from which to date they have been virtually excluded?

By establishing very close social bonds with animals, some scientists are at last beginning to prove the consciousness of animals more deeply and effectively than ever before. Dr. John Lilly has made some remarkable discoveries in his communication studies with dolphins as have the Gardners with Washoe (who learned over 130 different signs and who invented some of her own) and other chimpanzees being taught to communicate using American Sign Language. Although it is beyond the scope and intention of this book to detail their research findings, it should be emphasized that it is remarkable what can be accomplished (with patience) once there is a close bond between experimenter and animal. With such a close bond, no experimenter can continue to perceive the animal as an unfeeling and irrational automaton. Through communicating with animals and exploring their consciousness, the investigator is *humanized* insofar as unfeeling, mechanistic attitudes toward nonhuman life are invalidated.

One anecdote from such research must be cited. A gorilla who had learned sign language was once asked which of the two keepers present he preferred. He signed back, "Bad question." One might infer from this that altruistic and egalitarian gorillas simply don't make such unfair social discriminations. While primates can be trained to make "if . . . then" logical inferences and to spontaneously make sign language sentences such as "Hurry, I want to go outside and play (or drive in the car or smell the flowers)," through this channel of communication researchers are also learning not only about their conceptual abilities, but also about their self-awareness and ethical/moral sensitivities.

Certain views are being advanced by academicians that are relevant to how we, as a society, relate to and treat animals and Nature. One such view is that humans are "superior" to other animals. Those who adhere to such a belief may be incapable of ethically objective and responsible action toward animals, because they perceive animals as inferior. With this preconceived notion that humans are superior (and that some animal species are more or less superior than others), the ethically objective principle of giving animals equal and fair consideration—which is a basic premise of animal rights philosophy—becomes anathema.

In apparent support of this view, Harvard University "sociobiologist" and science popularizer Edward O. Wilson has constructed a list of the ten most intelligent animals. *The Book of Lists* (New York: William Morrow, 1983), in its section on the animal kingdom, reproduced the following:

DR. EDWARD O. WILSON'S
10 MOST INTELLIGENT ANIMALS
1. Chimpanzee (two species)
2. Gorilla
3. Orangutan
4. Baboon (seven species, including drill and mandrill)
5. Gibbon (seven species)
6. Monkey (many species, especially macaques, the patas, and the Celebes black ape)
7. Smaller toothed whale (several species, especially killer whale)
8. Dolphin (many of the approximately 80 species)
9. Elephant (two species)
10. Pig

Dr. Wilson adds: "I defined intelligence as the speed and extent of learning performance over a wide range of tasks. Insofar as possible, the rank ordering was based in part on actual experiments conducted on learning ability. In those cases where such studies have not been made, I relied on the 'encephalization index,' which measures the size of the brain relative to that of the body as a whole and has been shown to be roughly correlated with intelligence. Although I believe that my rank ordering is relatively sound, much more research is needed in this field of zoology, and changes in position can easily occur, especially near the bottom of the list of 10."

It should be pointed out, however, that "speed and extent of learning performance over a wide range of tasks," and the "encephalization index" are arbitrary, not absolute, indices of intelligence. Comparing the learning performance and brain size relative to body size of different species sets up absolute differences between species. And when a hierarchy is drawn up, a further erroneous inference is made, namely that of superiority.

This "speciesist" thinking is a reflection of our own values, especially of our valuing intelligence as some special virtue. Such valuation can distort our perceptions of other animals and influence how we treat them and value them in and for themselves. A "dumb beast," low in the sapience or IQ hierarchy, would not be accorded the same respect as a more intelligent species (that is, one "more human" in some respects). Yet all animals should be respected equally, since they are all sentient, having the capacity to feel and to suffer.

While comparing different species is one avenue to understanding evolution, adaptation and the structure and function of living things, making comparisons on the basis of biased, human-centered values can have pernicious ramifications. Any hierarchy (of superior to inferior or greater to lesser) sets up a false view of reality, and when it is imposed upon the animal kingdom, it can break the circle of compassion within which all creatures should be regarded and treated with equal reverence and respect.

That Professor Wilson listed the chimpanzee first and not *Homo sapiens* is his first biological error. But it is, I believe, a politically coercive, if not unconscious, omission. It would seem by this omission that Wilson would have us believe that we are so superior to all other animals that we do not rank with them. Yet are we not, along with the gorilla and orangutan, less intelligently adapted to life in the water than a dolphin (which he ranks eighth)? And is not a tenth-ranking pig more intelligent at being a pig, and living in its own particular environmental niche, than a dolphin or a chimpanzee could ever be?

What is Professor Wilson doing? Other biologists before him placed Negro and European and Asiatic peasant races beneath their white, Anglo-Saxon Protestant ideal of superiority and human perfection. With such an arrogant attitude of patriarchal supremacy over others and the rest of creation, no ethical decision could be objective and unbiased. All moral choices would be made by some arbitrary consensus of reality and of our supreme place in Nature that would be ultimately self-serving. Wilson's animal IQ hierarchy sets up the pyramid of power. Is it not as speciesist as his predecessor biopoliticians were racist?

Then there is philosopher Mortimer Adler, whose books, like biologist Wilson's, present the speciesist view of man's superiority over the animal kingdom as irrefutable truth. His writings have wide public appeal and have been lauded by educators, though other philosophers generally ignore his pontifications.

In many of his writings he has argued that rationality is the highest virtue, and since man is the only truly rational being on Earth, he is superior to the rest of creation and thus there is nothing morally wrong in his exploiting animals.

In his most recent popular book, *Ten Philosophical Mistakes*, he supports the views of Thomas Aquinas, who derived his philosophy from Aristotle and incorporated it into Christian theology, reasoning, for example, that only rational beings (humans) have immortal souls. Animals are therefore inferior. So naturally, Adler is critical of Charles Darwin (who was cognizant of animals' emotions and was concerned about their widespread mistreatment, especially by vivisectors) for classifying man as an animal. Professor Adler contends that man alone can conceive of right and wrong. Thus man is a superior being, capable of moral responsibility and ethical conduct. However, we, unlike animals, have the power of free will to act immorally and unethically, so does this not make us "inferior" to other animals? That it is in our best interests to be morally right and ethically responsible is a sign of enlightened self-interest, not of superiority over the animal kingdom. It is worth noting that Adler stresses the difference in sapience of man over animals that makes him superior, rather than emphasizing (as did Darwin) the similarities in sentience—in emotional reactions and feelings—that make us feel kinship and compassion rather than superiority.

It should be emphasized that many opponents of animal rights philosophy have argued that only humans can have rights because only humans can act as moral agents. Nonrational animals, having no sense of right and wrong, cannot therefore have rights. But since babies and comatose patients, who are neither rational nor capable of being moral agents, have rights, because they are recognized as "moral objects," it is illogical not to regard animals also as objects of moral concern with interests and therefore rights. Adler's thinking leads to the opposite conclusion, denying animals their rights.

In contrast to the unfeeling, "mechanomorphic" view of animals described earlier, the more sentimentally *anthropomorphic* "animals are little people" attitude may seem more logical and humane. But such an attitude can be just as bad (for the animals) as the mechanistic view. The anthropomorphic view can lead to excessive pampering and overindulgence that may be physically or psychologically bad for a pet. Very often a lonely person, or one who feels alienated from his or her own kind, will make a pet into a substitute for a human companion or a substitute child. The owner may project all kinds of attributes upon the pet, verging on illusory and sometimes delusory notions. A wide range of emotions and thought processes that it simply does not have may be attributed to the pet. Even the animal's normal behavior (such as growling "leave me alone") may be grossly misinterpreted (in this case as a "you don't love me anymore" response). Such excessive subjectivity in relation to the person's perception of an animal is clearly as unhealthy and as potentially detrimental to the well-being and "rights"

Today we know more about dogs than ever before. We know more about their bodies and how to maintain their health and battle illness. We know about their psychological makeup—what triggers a host of responses and how to make the most of them for the sake of the human-canine bond. But friends of dogs should remember that not everyone shares their views, and that some would like to limit their right to the pleasure of canine companionship. With all our enhanced knowledge, we should also remember to exercise responsibility regarding our pets in a world where they are not always appreciated.

Photo courtesy HSUS/Hegedus

of the animal as is the overly objective and detached mechanistic attitude. Neither form of relationship appreciates the intrinsic worth of the animal.

We should also remember that many pets will learn to manipulate, indeed train their owners to get what they want. Many cats and dogs have succeeded in training their owners to feed them only salmon or filet mignon, and are able to have most, if not all, their needs gratified—an owner may ignore guests to attend to the pet (who is jealous), or a husband and wife may sleep in separate rooms because the dog has decided not to let husband sleep with wife. Some pets will even pretend to be sick—for example, by feigning an injured paw—in order to get their owner's attention. We should, therefore, never underestimate the intelligence of our pets and above all, never cease to regard them as being different from ourselves in terms of their individuality. We should respect and understand this "otherness" of the animals in our lives, and not, through anthropomorphic thought and action, try to make them seem more human than they naturally are. If we did, the significance of their "otherness" would be diluted and they might well be swallowed up in the sameness of anthropocentrism, a world in which pets are mere artifacts, human creations that have no individuality, but are merely extensions of ourselves. Let us preserve in our minds and lives their uniqueness and animalness, for on the other side of our "oneness" with Nature and animals is the reality of their "otherness."

We can do more than simply feed, groom and play with our pets. We can begin by respecting them, not as our own creations or property, but in a manner more in line with the sentiment so eloquently expressed by Henry Beston in *The Outermost House* (New York: Ballantine Books, 1971):

> We need another and wiser and perhaps a more mystical concept of animals. Remote from universal nature, and living by complicated artifice, man in civilization surveys the creature through the glass of his knowledge and sees thereby a feather magnified and the whole image in distortion. We patronize them for their incompleteness, for their tragic fate of having taken form so far below ourselves. And therein we err, and greatly err. For the animal shall not be measured by man. In a world older and more complete than ours they move finished and complete, gifted with extensions of the senses we have lost or never attained, living by voices we shall never hear. They are not brethren, they are not underlings; they are other nations, caught with ourselves in the net of life and time, fellow prisoners of the splendour and travail of the earth.

Also, as we respect them, so we can explore their intelligence and consciousness, educate them and help them realize their potential under our custodianship. In the process, we will be educating ourselves, and by so doing, we will gain a deeper understanding of and reverence for our animal companions. Let us liberate them from the status of objects and property, from the tyranny of utilitarian exploitation and from the need to use them for selfish emotional gratification, all at their expense.

In animal liberation is also our own liberation, and as we begin to appreciate the intelligence and sensitivity of our companion animals, the day will come when they will be accorded the respect and rights that for too long they have been denied.

Even after centuries of intimate association with our own species, the dog's responses still mirror those of his ancestor, the wolf. Pack forming and denning all trace back to a dog's feral roots, and those roots often hold the clues to canine intelligence. *Photo courtesy HSUS*

The best hope for the development of respect for all life lies in our children. When children are encouraged to regard dogs and other animals as sentient beings rather than living distractions, they are likely to develop into compassionate adults. *Photo courtesy HSUS*

16

IQ Tests (Games and Exercises) for Dogs

THE IQ TESTS and exercises in this book have been developed so that people can not only evaluate their dog's IQ through the testing procedures, but also teach the animal something new. Consequently, its IQ will be improved and its conceptual and experiential world enriched.

There are also advantages to the owner and to the owner's relationship with the dog. A greater appreciation and understanding of the dog will come after observing and working with it. Dogs need more than petting, feeding, cleaning and exercising. They need to be educated and entertained. Their lives can be enriched with IQ tests, and such learning experiences are rewarding games that can be enjoyed by the whole family.

It does concern me that many dogs are often kept like household plants or toys that are fed, watered and occasionally played with. They can and should be given much more, and the more their lives are enriched with constructive IQ test games, the more our lives will be enriched with a deeper rapport with and appreciation for our nonhuman companions.

This is, I believe, especially important for children. Being exposed to animals in childhood can give them a greater understanding of and reverence for life.

A child involved in observing, testing and teaching his or her pet, using some of the IQ test procedures described in this book, will soon learn that dogs are intelligent creatures.

Domestication has lowered the general intelligence and awareness of some of the animals we keep as pets. We should not demean them for this, since it was our doing in the first place. Some of the reasons behind the simplification and decline in behavior, intelligence and other traits as a consequence of domestication have been discussed earlier.

It is my hope that dog shows will place less emphasis on looks and performance in obedience trials and stress more the importance of stability of temperament and the development of IQ, both of which can be tested objectively. Imagine how such tests could help improve the quality of many breeds. There *are* canine geniuses. People can do more than simply select and breed dogs for good looks and obedience.

All of the tests in this book are humane if done properly and require no surgical, drug or other "experimental" manipulation or intervention to alter the animal in some way. The scientifically minded student looking for a suitable (and humane) science fair project with an animal will find a variety of projects in this book.

Finally, the patience and understanding of the tester or educator are crucial. One who pushes the animal too hard, gives up easily or becomes frustrated and angry when the pet does not give the right response will have a significant negative effect on the animal's performance.

PRINCIPLES AND CONCEPTS

Before embarking upon a detailed description of IQ tests and IQ-enhancing lessons and games for pets, a foundation of basic principles and key concepts should first be laid out. Once you understand some of the essential aspects of learning theory and practice, you can avoid mistakes and misinterpretations in the execution and evaluation of IQ tests.

First, let us consider *intelligence.* It is essentially the capacity to acquire and store information and to use such information (or knowledge) at some later time. Acquisition is a function of *learning ability,* which in turn is influenced by several factors. Performance

172

may be affected by *motivation*—in other words, by how keen the animal is to perform and learn. Hunger, fear, praise and fatigue may influence motivation, either singly or together and either positively or negatively. An animal that is motivated to perform well in order to receive food or praise is likely to learn better than one that is not hungry or is afraid.

Motivation is affected not only by the animal's internal physiological and emotional states, but also by various *reinforcing* factors. Positive reinforcers include food reward and praise; negative reinforcement may entail punishment or lack of food reward.

For the best results, the physiological and emotional state of the animal should be as stable or as predictable as possible throughout all trials. If such is not the case, reinforcement may not be effective. For example, an animal that is not hungry or is too afraid may refuse food reinforcement. It will therefore have low motivation, its performance will be poor and any inferences about its learning ability and IQ would be inaccurate.

In many intelligence tests and problem tasks, the animal may get rewarded in other ways. Certain actions—manipulation, exploration and even play—can be rewarding in themselves. This is called *self-reinforcement;* it is the enthusiasm of a subject who is eager to perform and to learn. Learning is coincidental to the task at hand, something which is often lacking in obedience training and in teaching (rather than educating) children in certain schools.

Various rewards may, therefore, operate in a learning task independent of the final consummatory reward and reinforcement of praise or food. Some "star" animals also seem to have a sense of satisfaction, if not accomplishment, in solving a particular problem. It should be remembered that *intermittent reinforcement* (not rewarding on a constant schedule) can motivate an animal more than constant reinforcement. Also, *positive reinforcement* is better, for animals and children alike, than punishment or negative reinforcement.

Many of the tests in this book entail hiding an object from the animal. The animal must then retrieve the object and sometimes remember where it was hidden. To a very poorly developed nervous system, an object that has disappeared and can therefore no longer be seen or smelled does not exist. It has "gone." That the average dog will seek out a hidden object (and even cache one itself and later retrieve it) shows that it has what is called *object consistency.* A subject must, therefore, have the ability to maintain a mental image of the object that has disappeared (that is, it must have imagination).

Psychologists refer to this as a *search image* (or *sollwert*). Without this ability, a bird would be less able to forage for insects under leaves and pebbles and a dog would have difficulty retrieving a bone it had buried in the garden.

Retention is another important aspect of intelligence. Some animals have poor ability to retain information. This is often, as with young animals, associated with a short *attention span,* the latter interfering with acquisition of information and with test performance.

Learning theorists have proposed that information that is learned not only must be retained (or stored, possibly as chemical RNA codes or *menmons*); it also must be retrieved. It is difficult to evaluate which may be deficient—retention or retrieval—when a learned response is not correctly executed. Evidence from brain stimulation studies with implanted electrodes in humans points to defective retrieval or recall in lapses in memory. While a multitude of experiences are filed away in the memory banks of the brain, only a relatively limited number can be spontaneously recalled.

One must also consider the animal's individual (idiosyncratic), breed and species limitations and specialized attributes. A rat, for example, is particularly adept at learning a maze or complex runway, while a squirrel may do better on a place-learning test (since it is not adapted to living in tunnels or runways, but is adept at caching and relocating food stores in various places). A dog has a superb sense of smell and could outperform any human being in tests involving this sense, while a test involving manual dexterity could place a rat over a cat and a cat over a dog. Such *motor* and *sensory limitations* and special *attributes* should always be kept in mind when considering intelligence and learning ability.

Once an animal has learned a given task or solved a particular problem, the next question is how long can it retain (or remember) what it has learned.

How long an animal can remember (or retain) a given learned response is another important facet of intelligence. Basically there are two forms of memory, called *short-* and *long-term memory.* An animal may remember a complex sequence of actions or certain cues or signals for several weeks or months: this is long-term memory. An example of short-term memory is a dog's remembering where a toy or morsel of food has been hidden in a test in which the reward may be concealed in one of two or more different places. Tests for long- and short-term memory will be described in the next chapter.

There are a number of interesting, revealing tests you can administer to your dog that will tell you a great deal about its intelligence. Such test results can help you do a better job of training and cement a more meaningful relationship with your pet.   *Photo courtesy HSUS/Marin County H.S.*

Behavior patterns spring from a variety of sources. Interaction between littermates helps identify dominant and submissive dogs and which ones will, upon maturity, make the most satisfactory companions, working dogs, hunters and show animals.

Sometimes recall can be aided by *association* or *déjà vu.* For example, a particular cue, in an otherwise completely new context, may trigger memories and a response elaborated earlier in association with a completely different set of cues. The similarity of certain past and present cues, by *association,* may not only aid recall but also enhance learning and the elaboration of some appropriate behavioral response. This is called *associative learning,* and is probably the most widespread form of learning in animals other than conditioning. For example, a simple connection between the presence of a particular person and receiving a food reward is conditioning, but anticipating a similar response from another person is associative learning. Learning here involves certain similarities between particular cues or classes of stimuli (in this case, different people). The development of generalized phobias is a good example of associative learning, as when fear of thunderstorms (or of uniformed policemen) generalizes into a fear of all sudden noises (or all uniformed people). The pattern here is one of responding to an increasing range of similar stimuli, which is called *stimulus generalization.*

Stimulus generalization in associative learning is also a normal aspect of learning, but the basic response pattern need not change. In other words, the response to a wide range of stimuli becomes habitual. While the response may be appropriate, *habit fixation* may limit the dog's ability to elaborate new or more appropriate responses. Many animals show such habit fixation and a relatively limited repertoire of responses. Species limitations are particularly evident, as are individual differences, as between one dog and another. One may continue to paw at a problem box while another may instead start to push with its nose or use its teeth. Perseverance and stereotypy of response in the first case contrasts with greater flexibility in the latter. The difference may be attributed to a greater freedom from habit fixation, which allows the animal a new dimension for further learning and adaptive modification of its behavior in problem solving.

This freedom from a fixed or limited repertoire of responses is the freedom to learn and to elaborate new and more adaptive responses. A strong-willed dog, one that verges on the obsessive compulsive, may perform well on a variety of problem tests, but on others will, like a person of similar temperament, fail miserably. Being too "headstrong," it may make more mistakes than a more cautious animal, and worse, may not have the "cool" to pause and try out a new and potentially more appropriate response.

An animal that does have self-control and can inhibit learned responses to try out new and more appropriate ones is free to learn. Without adequate self-control or *internal* inhibition (as in a young animal, one that is overexcited or headstrong), reasoning and insight may be impaired.

Pavlov, in his conditioning studies with dogs, identified three basic temperament types. He ascribed a "weak and unstable nervous typology" to those dogs who had a timid temperament and were easily distracted and disturbed during tests. Those dogs that performed well on those tests requiring action, but did poorly on tests that required inaction (passivity or inhibition), were said to have a "strong but imbalanced nervous typology." (These are the headstrong temperaments alluded to earlier.) Pavlov's third type, his superdogs, did equally well on tests requiring action or inhibition: they had a "strong and balanced nervous typology." The ability to appropriately switch their behavior he termed *equilibration* or *dynamism.*

What these landmark studies reveal is that temperament influences learning ability and IQ. To say that genes (inheritance) influence intelligence is too long a leap: the intervening factor is temperament or emotionality. While temperamental traits are inherited, it has been shown earlier in this book how *early experiences* (the way in which an animal is raised) can help an animal develop a more stable and adaptable temperament. Good breeding alone will not produce intelligent animals.

Another important and subtle aspect of intelligence testing is determining the animal's ability to *unlearn* a given response pattern. This is an indicator of flexibility, not so much of insight as of the animal's capacity to control response perseverance or stereotypy. For example, an animal that persists in looking for food in one place where food has been hidden earlier and cannot "switch off" its place preference and locate food hidden in another place is showing poor flexibility and high stereotypy or perseverance. A dog who continues to look for food under a card marked "X" when the food is now placed under card "O" is also showing maladaptive perseverance. The animal is unable to inhibit or "unlearn" its response and will always expect food to be under the "X" card. The ability to reverse behavior to different cues, as when one cue is first positive or rewarding and later negative or nonrewarding, is a good indicator of intelligence. Such an animal, in Pavlov's terminology, has dynamism or equilibration.

Four other types or patterns of learning remain to be described. One that is used for many of the IQ tests and for IQ development in this book is *learning sets.* With learning sets, the animal essentially learns to learn. Through paced increments of experiences, the subject learns to master more and more difficult problems that are based upon the same learning principles. For example, learning to discriminate between different shapes or symbols can lead to discrimination between different groups of symbols or words until the animal is actually able to "read."

A common learning pattern in all but the least intelligent pets is *time-event learning.* The pet learns to anticipate certain occurrences during the day and through conditioning and association comes to know what its owner is going to do next. The animal will pattern many of its behaviors after the owner's activities, such as waking up and anticipating being fed, exercised and groomed. This is not difficult since most animals (including man) are creatures of habit. Changes in such routines can upset some animals and may actually interfere with IQ tests. For example, it would be unwise to put an animal through its paces just after it has eaten or when it is anticipating a daily romp outdoors.

Many animals, especially cats, have the capacity for *observational learning.* After seeing their owner or another animal doing something, they may attempt to do the same. Also termed *mimic learning,* this capacity is highly evolved in the more intelligent animals such as humans and chimpanzees and is an important key to the acquisition of cultural knowledge, which is literally passed on from one generation to the next via observation and imitation.

Sometimes an animal may, in its behavior, display clearly rational and logical intent. *Insight* or *reasoning ability* are not purely human attributes. More highly evolved animals can also make insightful decisions and make logical "if . . . then" inferences. For example, a dog may push a stool over to enable it to reach up to obtain a food reward that would otherwise be out of reach. Observational learning may help an animal execute such an insightful solution, much like a young chimpanzee observing an older one using a trimmed twig to "fish" for termites. The observer, in copying, is making a logical inference: "If I do this, then I too should be rewarded."

BASIC PET IQ AND TEMPERAMENT TESTS

There are several simple tests that you can put your dog through to evaluate its IQ. Some of the tests are games that your pet

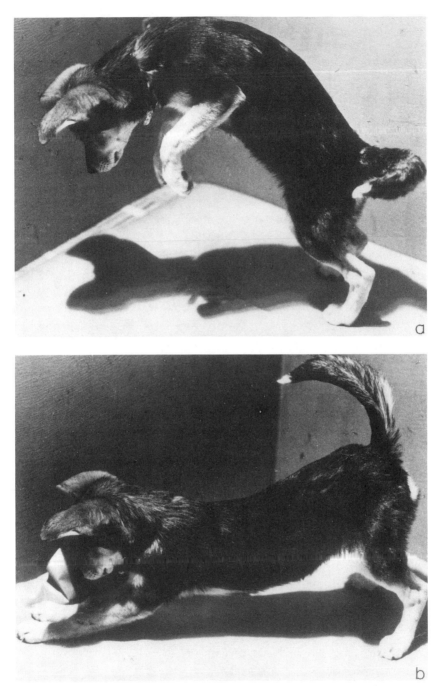

Playful leaping behaviors in a coyote/dog hybrid: a) pounce with a four-limb stab; b) alternative interpretation of the play bow that may be derived from the latter action.   *Photo courtesy HSUS*

will enjoy, and by conducting them, you may actually increase your pet's IQ by helping it learn to learn. But there are two great obstacles to be overcome before any such tests are attempted. First, there is the human problem. Only those people who are patient and who don't get frustrated easily should do these tests. If you are in too much of a rush or get frustrated when your dog doesn't respond or responds incorrectly, it will pick up your reactions and will become even more confused and frustrated.

The second obstacle is your dog's temperament. You should know its temperament before you try the IQ tests, because temperament has a profound influence upon performance. An animal that is afraid or uninterested won't score well. A poor performance does not therefore mean that you have a "dumb" dog, but rather, you or its temperament (or a combination of the two) are interfering with its performance. Knowing how to evaluate an animal's temperament can also help you pick out the best puppy in a litter, since research has shown that by six to ten weeks of age the basic temperament that a dog will have as an adult is already well formed.

Temperament Tests

These tests can be done on puppies from six to eight weeks of age onward. In computing a puppy's rating, simply put down the appropriate score for each test and add them up. A very *high score* means a strong-willed and outgoing animal; a *low score* means a shy, fearful animal. A *mid* to *high grade score* is probably the best, since such a dog would be outgoing but at the same time cautious and not foolhardy. These three basic "grades" correspond to Pavlov's three basic dog temperaments or "nervous typologies" (the strong, weak and balanced types respectively).

Social Responsiveness

a. When called, does the dog solicit your attention (10), approach you slowly and quietly greet you (5) or shy away (2)? (Note the number shown in parentheses and continue with the other tests, noting for each item the appropriate number for the response that the animal gives.)

b. If the puppy is with its littermates, does it push its way out first over its littermates to contact you (10), come up with one or two others to investigate you (5) or stay back and ignore you (2)?

Scientific research has shown that by six to ten weeks of age, a puppy's basic adult temperament is already well formed. This knowledge enables us to identify personality types in a litter and to work with very young puppies to make the most of the puppy's temperament. *Percy T. Jones*

c. When petted or picked up, does the puppy get overexcited (10), remain quiet and relaxed (5) or freeze fearfully, tremble or try to escape (2)?

d. When you quietly back away, does the puppy follow you immediately and solicit attention (10), pause and then follow you and solicit your attention less demonstratively (5) or go off and ignore you (2)?

e. Call the puppy toward you and when it is beside you, clap your hands loudly twice over its head. Then call it to come to you. Does it ignore the loud noise and continue to solicit your attention (10), cower or become passive and recover quickly (5), or freeze and refuse to approach even when you try to coax it (2)?

f. How does the puppy respond to certain toys? (Dogs are generally less playful as adults, so this test can give false measures with more inhibited or "cool" adults.) Use a yard of string with a four-inch piece of towel or paper tied to the end. Drag it past the puppy as though it were a mouse hopping by. Score (10) for an immediate response, (5) if the dog paws tentatively or crouches and stalks first and (2) for no response other than looking at the "prey" or simply ignoring it.

g. How does the puppy respond in an unfamiliar place, say outside its kennel or home, in a park or quiet yard? Does it explore actively but with some caution (10), does it freeze, cower or attempt to hide somewhere (2) or does it run around wildly exploring things and not calm down quickly (5)?

Since my research has shown a relationship between heart rate and temperament in pups, you may wish to try to detect heart rate with a stethoscope. Pups with the highest resting heart rates in the litter tend to be the most assertive and outgoing, while those with the lowest rates are the most timid. The same may hold true for kittens, but this has not yet been researched. Simply hold the puppy in your lap and when it is quiet and not struggling, record its heartbeats for fifteen seconds; multiplying by four gives you the rate per minute. Outgoing pups have rates of 200–240 beats per minute, while others in the same litter having rates as low as 160–180 per minute will as adults most likely be shy and easily frightened by sudden or unfamiliar stimuli. Those, then, will be the poor learners.

Since the above temperament tests require the presence of a person, which could bias the tests and lead to incorrect inferences, other tests without a person present are essential. So repeat test (g) with yourself concealed behind a blind or suitable screen. Next throw some large and unusual object near the puppy, such as a ball of paper or a cardboard box about the same size as the animal. This way you can test its reactions to *surprising* and *novel stimuli.* Other setups include a string pulley that suddenly pops up a cardboard shape in front of the animal, or approaching the animal and opening a large umbrella. Score (10) for an unhesitating approach, (5) for cautious approach or withdrawal, then investigation, and (2) for flight with no investigation.

Also observe how the puppy reacts, in your apparent absence, to others that it lives with or to its littermates. Score (10) if it is always number one when playing with others or in getting food, (5) if it is intermediate and (2) if it is obviously the lowest one on the totem pole.

The above simple tests can help you select a pup that will have a stable temperament, which in turn will be amenable to training and IQ evaluation. Don't forget, either, that training and IQ testing is much easier if your pet is strongly attached to you. If it has not been properly socialized you may not get much further than simply evaluating its temperament.

We can do much more with our companion animals than cater to their basic needs and train them to be obedient; we can, to a degree, actually educate them and develop their IQs. Scoring their responses and computing their IQs is part of the game for us: for them, the enjoyable part is having human attention and engaging in a variety of problem-solving games. This is one way we can be closer to them and enrich their lives, and in so doing, help develop potential that is usually dormant because of the bland, unstimulating world we so often keep them in.

HOW TO SCORE

Each of the following tests consists of five trials. For each correct trial, score 10, for each total failure, score 0 and for a slower, confused response that does eventually come out right, score 5. Add the scores for each trial, multiply by four and you have an "IQ rating." Out of a possible 200, anything above 125 is superior, anything above 150 near genius. A score around 50 isn't so hot and below that, you may have goofed in conducting the tests or your subject may have been emotionally disturbed, simply not motivated or brain damaged!

HIDE AND SEEK

This test is based upon the notion that when an object disappears from view, it can still be visualized or held in the animal's memory. This is termed object consistency. As with most of these tests, it is advantageous to have a helper who gently restrains the animal until you are ready for it to respond. You may wish to first "shape" your pet to retrieving or at least finding the toy by throwing it various places in the room. Once you have a consistent response pattern (say five out of five), place the toy halfway under an old towel (crinkly newspaper may scare the animal) and repeat this once or twice. Praise the animal each time it responds correctly. Finally, place the toy completely under the towel and see what happens. A bright dog should be able to get the toy a few seconds after it is released by your helper. Don't do any more tests now until the following day, or your pet may soon tire of this game and give an erroneous low score.

Next day "show" the toy to your pet, who is being quietly restrained about eight to ten feet away. Place the toy under the towel and then back off to one side and signal your helper to release the animal. Repeat this test five times and calculate its IQ rating.

HIDDEN FOOD

Because not all dogs will be motivated to find a hidden toy, the hide-and-seek test should be compared with your pet's ability to find hidden food. Show it some tasty morsel of food, place the food on a flat plate and hide it under the towel. Do this test about one hour before your dog's normal feeding time. If you test it at the usual feeding time, its habitual expectation of being fed (at the usual place and time) could interfere with this test, and, of course, after feeding the pet may not be in the least bit interested in responding. The animal should make every effort to remove the towel and get at the food beneath it. Repeat this test five times and do not give it more than a quarter teaspoonful of food each time, or it may get satiated too quickly. Comparing the results of this test with those of the first one will give you a good idea how food-motivated your pet is. A high score on this test can compensate for a low score on the first for an animal that isn't "turned on" by some toy object.

These two tests form the basis of several more advanced tests that may be conducted once you are able to get your pet to respond with a high degree of consistency. Because the animal may be able to see the shape of the toy under the towel, or smell it and the food, the next sequence of tests is designed to make things a little more difficult.

RECOGNIZING THE CHANGE

Wild animals that I have studied are extremely sensitive to changes in their familiar surroundings. Any novel object, a cardboard box, ball, balloon, crumpled pile of wrapping paper, and so forth, will trigger an immediate response: sudden attention, flight or cautious approach and investigation. Such animals are highly aware of their environment, and such awareness can be easily measured in our pets. With the dog in another room, place some completely new object in the middle of the living-room floor, such as a large balloon or a small opened umbrella. Don't handle it much or handle it with tongs since your own scent could reduce its novelty. Then sit back and wait and see what your dog does when it comes in. For no response, score 0, for a brief look, score 5 and for a clear, orienting response, cautious or immediate approach and investigation, score 10.

THE "TUBE" TEST

This is a special "cat and mouse" test that is very appropriate for cats and for most dogs as well. Get a cardboard tube about two and a half to three feet long with a three-inch diameter. Attach a small toy or morsel of meat to a string and pull it through the tube. Let your pet see it disappear into the hole at one end, and see you pull it out at the other end. Keep at least four feet away from this end of the tube. Your pet should quickly learn to come to the end nearest you to wait for the "mouse" to appear. Score 10 for a quick grasp of the spatial concept, 5 if you have to repeat it more than five times and 0 if your pet stays by the end of the tube where the "mouse" first disappeared. Having an assistant pull on the string at the point of entry into the tube can speed up this test. Then the meat or toy must be tied to the middle of a long length of string.

The cardboard cylinder can also be used for the more advanced "tool" using test in Chapter 17, in which the food or toy is pulled into the tube out of reach of the pet except for a wire loop or wooden toggle that the pet must pull on to pull the reward from inside the tube.

RIGHT AND LEFT

Use two cake (baking) tins and a cardboard box to cover the front of each tin. Your dog has access to either tin via the back of the box, which is open. Set the tins about three feet apart inside their boxes and show the animal in which box you are placing the toy. After the dog has made two correct responses, switch over and use the opposite box. It should not persist in going to the wrong box. Once you have accustomed your pet to this test with five or six trials, wait twenty-four hours and then test its IQ. Do five tests, placing the toy alternately in one box (A), then the other box (B), in the following pattern: A, B, A, B and finally B. This last repetition will show you whether the animal has developed a spontaneous A–B alternation, rather than solving the problem.

Repeat the above tests using a minute amount of the dog's favorite food. Smear each tin with a little of the food dissolved in water first to be sure the dog is not simply responding to odor cues. If the pet gives a wrong response on any of these trials, do not allow it to go near the other tin. Simply return it to your helper, and remove the food or toy from the tin, hold it up for the animal to see and then place it in the next-in-sequence box, and when ready signal your pet to be released. For this test it is necessary to stand close to the boxes to prevent your pet from going immediately from one box to the next, unless you wish to make the boxes out of wood and have a guillotine door on the back that you can open or close at a distance with rope and pulley.

It is worth spending plenty of time on this test, because once an animal does understand what it is supposed to do, several more advanced tests can be built upon this one.

FRUSTRATION-DEXTERITY

Once your dog knows which box the toy or food is behind, the next test is to frustrate the animal by putting the food or toy on the ground with the tin inverted over it. Each tin should have one lip bent outward so that the animal can get a paw or nose under it. A dexterous animal who thinks first and doesn't give up easily or become overly frustrated and paw frantically at the tin should quickly solve this problem. Again, give five trials on one day and repeat the next day, giving five trials and scoring each successful response.

FRUSTRATION-DETOUR

For this test, you need a barricade of chicken-wire, or a couple of chairs with low crossbars on the legs that the animal can't get under. Place or throw the toy or food on one side of the barrier and then release the animal on the other side to go get it. Some head-strong dogs will crash unthinkingly into the barrier. Those having more insight will immediately go around one side or the other. Repeat this test five times and record the number of correct responses. Repeat the next day with one side of the barrier blocked by a wall (put the chicken-wire barrier or edge of one chair securely right up against the wall). The dog should immediately go to the open side, or correct itself after one mistake. After the second trial, remove the existing block and block the other side if possible. (A corridor in the house is ideal for this reversal test.)

SOCIABILITY AND DETOUR

The frustration-detour test can be conducted on pups to evaluate their sociability and intelligence. Place the animal on one side of the barrier, step back and call it to come to you. Repeat the test five times after praising the animal each time it solves the detour and comes to you. An excessively aroused and distressed animal will at first keep pushing and pawing at the middle of the barrier to reach you. It should eventually solve the problem (keep both sides of the barrier open) and when placed back behind the barrier should come round with little further delay. Start scoring only once the animal has come to you on its own on the first trial, and give five trials. Next day, repeat five times and then block one end, selecting that end first which the animal may favor coming around. If it is "stuck," show it the way out once only and do five trials. The dog should not persist in trying to get through the blocked edge of the barrier. Then do another five trials with the other edge against the wall. On the third day, you can test the animal's ability to alternate its behavior by alternately blocking each end of the barrier (A, B, A, B, B).

Score 0 each time the dog cannot solve the detour problem, give 10 for an immediate correct response and 5 if it takes more than twenty seconds to come or if it tries to get through one blocked end first. Five trials will then give you a total of 50. Multiply this by four and you will have a rough score of the animal's IQ. A score anywhere over 150 means you have a very intelligent and sociable animal companion.

FRUSTRATION-INSIGHT

For this test, take your dog out on a long leash. Loop the leash around a tree or post with yourself on one side and the dog on the other, in such a way that if the dog comes to you in a straight line, the leash will bring him up short. Call the dog to you and see if he solves the problem. He will at first try to come straight to you, but he should quickly figure out why he can't and go around behind the tree to free himself. If he can't do it and gets tangled up, let go of the leash and repeat the test later, showing him how to solve the problem. A dog that gets a clear five trials right the first time is a genius. One that learns after ten to twenty trials is average, and one that never learns has problems. Many dogs that are too owner-attached try desperately to reach the owner and get tangled up or helplessly give up and wait to be helped out. Overdependence and helplessness and overemotional, hysterical reactions do interfere with this and other tests and they are certainly deterrents to an animal's exercising its learning ability.

188

In many instances, types—and later specific dog breeds—came into being in response to certain needs. The ancestors of these Border Terriers were naturally rugged and capable of independent action in order to keep small predators like foxes and weasels in check in the English/Scottish border districts. *John L. Ashbey*

17

Advanced IQ Tests and Exercises

THERE ARE several more advanced tests and lessons that can be given to your dog once the tests described in the previous chapter have been completed.

"TOOL" USING

It is possible to train dogs to use a wire loop or piece of string with a stick "handle" as a "tool" in order to obtain food. What is needed is a gate (an expandable baby gate set up in an open doorway), the bottom bar of which is four inches or so off the ground. Place the dog on one side and a low pie tin containing a small quantity of the dog's favorite food on the other. Let the wooden handle lie on the dog's side of the gate, with the other end, with the wire loop or string, attached to the pie tin. Staying on the pet's side of the barrier, show it how to pull the tin under the barrier, and do this for five days at the usual feeding time. On the sixth day, let the dog attempt to do it itself. Score 10 for an immediate response, 5 if it tries but fails and 0 if it does nothing. Many pets will get the hang of this very quickly because they are naturally good learners through observation.

Before you do this test, you may want to check your dog's *insight and spatial sense*. Have it chase a ball or other toy you throw for it across the room, then throw it *under* the barrier. If your pet runs headlong into the barrier the first time, but solves the problem the second time, score 5. If it runs into it again the next time you throw the toy, score 0. If it immediately pulls up short and tries to reach under the barrier on the first test, score 10.

SHORT-TERM MEMORY

The following test is called the delayed response test and is excellent for measuring your dog's short-term memory. Two boxes and two cake tins are needed for this. Show the dog behind which box you have placed the toy or food in the cake tin and then have your helper cover the dog's eyes with one hand. Its vision should be occluded for five seconds, then the dog can be released and allowed to choose the correct box. Do not allow the animal to correct any mistake *ever* in any of these tests. After it has made correct responses, the next day cover its eyes for ten seconds, and subsequently for even longer periods. A very intelligent dog can probably retain the image of the "correct" tin for up to five minutes. Score 10 for anything over two minutes, 5 for a delay of fifteen seconds to two minutes and 0 for any time of less than fifteen seconds.

VISUAL DISCRIMINATION

For this test, put a large "X" or other symbol on one box and a large "O" on another, and train the animal to go to the "X" marked box in order to get its reward. Reverse the positions of the boxes so your pet doesn't get a right or left side preference and instead has to read the signs. Once you have trained it to do this, you may then switch it to respond to the "O" card. Gradually you will, in this way, be educating your pet to respond to visual symbols, and you can build its repertoire with a whole range of different cards. One trainer actually taught his dog to read a variety of different cards, and the dog did learn to recognize the word "FOOD." This could be the key to teaching our pets to "read"—given plenty of time and patience.

Once you have your dog running to the correctly marked box, since it sees you putting food inside the box, it may still be responding primarily to you and not to the symbol. The first step, therefore, should be to give the animal five trials and let it see you put the food behind, say, the box marked "X" each time. Reverse the position of the two boxes for each trial: XO, OX, XO, XO, OX.

Then you must see if the dog has learned that "X" means food and will only go to the "X" marked box. You can accomplish this by having your assistant block the dog's view as you place food behind box "X" and then switch the position of the boxes. Give five trials and allow the dog to correct its mistake if it goes to the wrong box. Then you are ready to give the test proper: five trials are allowed and this time the dog is not allowed to correct itself. Keep score, and repeat the trials the next day.

A sophisticated improvement of this test can be constructed by providing a sliding guillotine door behind each box, operated by a pulley system. Keep the doors open during the first five trials, then keep them closed during the next five. Gently pull the door open on the correct box when the dog goes to it, even after going to the wrong box first. Then when you run the actual test, keep both doors closed and open the correct one only when your pet goes straight to it. Don't forget to switch the position of the boxes between trials. This may sound complicated, but once you have learned how to do it, it will go very smoothly indeed.

You can make all kinds of variations on this test. Make it more difficult and advanced by using three cake tins with boxes, with two marked the same ("X" and "X") and the other marked "O." The dog must learn only to approach the odd ("O") box in order to get rewarded. Again, change the positions of the boxes to insure your pet isn't developing a position or place preference. Once your dog gets the hang of this, you can draw all kinds of different symbols for this oddity discrimination test. If you are a carpenter, make some wooden cubes, pyramids and hexagons of different sizes, rest a set of three on plywood boards over three cake tins and you are on your way to evaluating just how well your pet can detect differences in shape, size and so on. The animal must learn to push the right object off the tin in order to get food.

In this kind of test, the dog is "learning to learn." The various trios of two similar and one odd shape serve as learning sets whereby the animal can learn to make finer and finer discriminations of size and shape differences.

You may wish to consider a slightly different setup for your

192

This dog shows evidence of discriminatory learning by its ability to retrieve food hidden under the appropriately lettered card. *Photo courtesy HSUS*

dog, using pie tins or plastic bowls not hidden behind a box but covered by a square of thin plywood or cardboard on which you put the appropriate symbol.

Begin first with an "X" card over one tin and train your dog to push the card over to get a minute food treat under it in the tin. You must first let it eat out of the tin before you cover it. Then your pet must learn to push the card away with its nose or paw. Next, add another tin with a blank card, and let it work itself through the problem until it has the concept that food is only under the "X" card. After this has been learned, alternate the positions of the tins randomly from left to right.

Subsequently you may elaborate upon this test by putting an "O" on the blank card and again only putting food under "X." Once your dog is giving an 80 to 100 percent correct response rate, switch the value of the signs so that "O" means food and "X" means an empty dish. Work slowly on this reversal, since some animals may have setbacks due to "overlearning" or being pushed too hard. With this kind of learning, it is essential that you do not spend too much time on it; about twenty minutes a day is usually all that your pet will take before becoming bored or frustrated. Also always have "school" at the same time each day.

When your pet is responding smoothly to this card game, you will be ready for further variations. You may add a third tin and train your dog to choose the odd symbol ("O," "X," "O") or have five or six tins with blank cards to test for place learning, as described above using boxes.

The beauty of using cards is that your dog has to perform by nosing or pawing the card, while with the box, it simply has to go around behind. With the cards, it is possible to train your pet to "read" and to "count." Begin with one card that has "DOG" written on it, while the tin next to it has a blank card. Say "dog" and point to the "DOG" card. Next put the word "CAT" or "FOOD" on the other and train your dog to switch as it did earlier from "X" to "O." In this way you can build up quite a vocabulary, and may eventually be able to set up three or four different cards and tell your pet to get "FOOD," "CHOW," "MEAT," "CAT," or "DOG." Similarly, you can teach it to count by putting one, two, three, four or more lines on each card. Remember it is probably easier for your pet if you say "one two three" for the number three card with three lines on it, and so on.

Using this card system, and much patience and ingenuity, trainer Elizabeth Mann Borgese actually taught her dog Arli to take dictation on a specially adapted electric typewriter. To what degree her dog was able to conceptualize is a moot point. There is clear evidence that pets do understand spoken words and through training can be conditioned to associate the spoken word (say "meat" or "chow") with a written symbol, be it the word *meat* or some representational symbol such as a triangle. Since it is easier to train pets to nose, paw or retrieve a card with some word or symbol on it than to teach them to speak, this technique may be the key to unlock the door that blocks factual and conceptual communication between us and our animal companions.

One day Arli was not feeling too well and didn't want to have his training session with Ms. Borgese. She reported that "Finally he put his nose to the A. I had dictated no A, but I thought I would let him do it anyway. He wrote, without any prompting and with all the spaces correct, *a bad a bad dog.* Did he mean it? . . . The case has remained isolated. . . . He hit the sequence by chance—a probability of about 1:12, or thereabouts. But it suited his state of mind. He 'meant' what he said."

Arli loved to ride in the car, and when asked "Arli, where do you want to go?" he would unfailingly write CAR, except that in his excitement he would "stammer" on the typewriter, and type out ACCACCAARR, GOGO CAARR.

Through word-associated conditioning, it should be possible to teach an intelligent dog to recognize such words as *dog, cat, cow, pig* and *horse,* and to teach it to recognize a picture of one of these animals and nose, paw or retrieve the appropriate word card. Ms. Borgese describes one dog, named Peg, who was able to do this. Washoe, the Gardners' chimpanzee, has been trained to give the right sign language for a variety of picture book objects. Even pigeons have been trained to respond to pictures only when human beings were present, sometimes making extremely fine judgments, identifying a human being that a person might not easily detect in the picture. These birds were responding on the basis of concept formation, not at a lower level of abstraction based upon simple geometric form.

We know that dogs can learn what *food, leash, walks, Where's your ball?* and other words mean, and that therefore they can acquire word-related concepts. They will, in their own way, develop their own unique "concepts," especially through original and often elaborate rituals such as jumping up and down when they want out, an action they originally perform at the door but later do in front of you. Other dogs will bring a leash or toy when they want to go out or to play. Since dogs are such acute observers, they are very responsive to the nonverbal body language cues that we give out, often unconsciously.

PLACE LEARNING

This is another short-term memory test, which requires the dog to remember behind which one of several boxes (or under which of several pie tins) you have placed the reward. The test is best done outdoors or in a large room. Make a semicircle of five or six boxes each about two to three feet away from the next. Show the animal behind which box (or under which tin) you have put the reward, and have your helper release your dog as soon as you stand up (but don't look at the box where the reward is). Most pets will make one or two errors to begin with, and this test, like the foregoing visual discrimination tests, are not easy to score to get an IQ scale. They are simply good learning experiences for your dog, and fun too. Once the animal has mastered the six box positions, you try variations, such as adding more boxes or placing the boxes only a foot apart. Be sure that if you are using food, you have each tin smeared with a little watery extract of the food, otherwise the dog may get the right tin on the basis of odor detection rather than visual place memory.

ODOR (SCENT)

There are many different scent tests that can be given to dogs. The important prerequisite is that your dog retrieve. Many of these tests are used in obedience trial competitions. A popular one is for the dog to pick out, from a variety of strange objects, the one object that has the odor of its owner, such as a glove or sock.

With a set of three or four objects, say a ball, glove, shoe and stick, it is possible to train a dog to retrieve any one of these objects when given the specific word *ball, shoe, stick* or *glove*. Begin with one object, then two, correcting the dog each time it makes a mistake. Many trainers have built up a large verbal repertoire for their dogs in this way, some having a clear understanding of forty or more specific words.

In advanced training of police and military dogs, it is not difficult to teach them to sniff out buried objects that smell of metal or explosives (money, land mines), concealed weapons or drugs. One way of training a dog to detect some drug or household spice is to stuff a sock or cloth bag with a little of the substance and train him to retrieve it. Then hide it some place in the room and tell him to go get it. Eventually, with the cue of a specific odor, the dog will immediately start to search for his "toy" whenever you say "Go get it."

SEARCH AND FIND

This test is used in advanced obedience training, where it is known as directed retrieving. One must first train a dog to retrieve objects. Then delay retrieving for a few seconds, walking the dog in a circle before you say "Go find it." Build up this delay time for as long as possible (say three to five minutes). The next stage is to drop some object, say a glove, which has your scent on it. Stand with the dog a few feet away, ideally with the object partially concealed in short grass. Make a throwing movement, then tell your dog "Go find it." If he can't, you must help him, get very close and let him retrieve it. Give lots of praise. You will soon have a dog who can find things you lose, and if he knows the appropriate word—glove, keys or whatever—so much the better!

REASONING AND INSIGHT

This test is for exceptionally promising dogs—and patient owners. It requires the dog to learn to move a box into the right position so that it can get on top of it to get a reward (with food or toy). First train the dog to sit on a sturdy, lightweight plywood box, and to stand on its hind legs to grab a morsel of food or favorite toy that is hanging above it on a piece of string. Once the dog has got the hang of this, move the box to one side, so that when he's on the box he can't reach the reward. Tell him to get down, then push the box over so he can get the reward. Repeat this several times and if he is a good observational learner, he will attempt to push the box into the right place when you suddenly stop helping him.

An alternative is to set up a gate across a doorway and arrange it so that the only way the dog can get over is by first standing on a box. Once he has learned this, move the box some distance away so he can't make it, then push the box closer so he can. Repeat this five or more times, then leave him to figure it out. A few more repetitions by you may be needed before he gets the hang of it or before you give up. Be sure that your dog is sufficiently agile and won't injure himself. The motivation to get over the gate could be either food reward or simply being called and given praise when he comes.

PUZZLE BOXES

If you are an ingenious as well as a patient kind of person, you can build a series of puzzle boxes for your dog—and entertain visitors too. First, build a box, say ten inches by fourteen inches by eight inches high, out of quarter- or half-inch wire netting so the animal can see into the box. Train it to go to the box and lift a loosely hinged lid to get whatever suitable reward you have put inside. Once the animal has mastered the trick of opening the wire "cage," you can next hide the reward inside a small cardboard box or wrap it in paper. Another complication is to put a catch on the lid, which the dog has to nose or paw up or to one side. Finally you can put a wooden peg in the catch which the dog has to pull out before it can move the latch.

Since dogs are dexterous, various devices can be put on the puzzle box to make it more and more difficult to open. One begins with the box open with food inside. Then close the lid, which the animal must learn to paw or nose open. Then add a toggle pin to close a latch on the lid, so that the animal must pull out the pin before lifting the lid. Learning can be accelerated through observation— that is, you can show your dog what to do. So far we have a three-part sequence. This can be made harder by adding one or two more toggle pins, an extra rope around the lid that has to be pulled off, and so on. All kinds of seemingly complex, but really rather simple sequences can be built up through this method. The extent is limited only by your interest and imagination and the understanding that IQ testing is not trick training.

If you are electronically minded, you may also wish to construct some operant conditioning systems for your pet. Many pets are good observers, dogs learning by themselves how to switch lights on, open doors, refrigerators and so forth. A low hanging string and toggle attached to a secure light fixture with a pull switch will entertain many pets who obviously enjoy switching the light on and off. A similar setup can be made for an instant-playing radio. If you know how to set up circuits with photo cells and pressure transducers, you could arrange it such that when your dog walks, sits or lies in a certain part of the room, a light, heat lamp, radio or TV goes on or off. Animals learn with remarkable speed that if they sit in one place, a radio or heat lamp will come on. More complex systems can be built involving operant conditioning and help enrich the animal's environment and give it a sense of control and relief from boredom.

Competitive obedience trials can bring out a dog's best physical abilities and potential for following direction while at the same time strengthening rapport with the owner. In the top photo, the dog executes a high jump in the process of returning the dumbbell to its handler. In the lower photo the dog, at the direction of the owner, will easily clear the broad jump.

Photo courtesy HSUS

Appendix:
Most Asked Questions About Dogs

$\mathbf{D}$OG OWNERS and would-be dog owners have one thing in common: questions about dogs. As a consequence of my writing and lecturing I get a constant deluge of questions, to the point where I see a pattern to the queries and problems. From this pattern I have chosen some of the most asked questions about dogs, which will help you understand and appreciate your dog or cope with certain problems better, as the case may be.

GENERAL HEALTH AND HABITS

First, some common questions about *general health*. The chronic coat-shedder is the bane of many dog owners. A dog with a dry, scruffy coat, which sheds constantly instead of with the seasons, makes a mess in the house and looks unkempt and uncared for. This problem would rarely occur in a dog that lived outdoors. Indoor living, especially in a heated house or apartment in the winter, will disrupt the normal coat growth and shedding cycle so that the coat is breaking out either constantly or intermittently. A common pattern is that of the dog who starts to grow a nice winter coat in early fall. Then the heat is turned on. The dog lies near a radiator, heater vent or fire and very soon you notice he's starting to shed. Some dogs get their seasonal coat cycles so messed up that when the heat is switched off in spring, they grow a thick coat better suited for the winter than the upcoming summer.

This problem is often complicated if the dog has a dry and sometimes scruffy coat. If your dog isn't a shedder and has this problem, follow the same advice as for a shedder. First give regular grooming to remove loose hair and scales and to distribute the natural oils evenly through the coat. A room humidifier will also help the dog and everyone in the household.

Dry and unkempt coats are often linked with feeding dry dog food or other commercial feeds that are low in polyunsaturated fats. Give your dog about one tablespoon per thirty pounds body weight of vegetable oil in its food every day. This will help some chronic shedders and many dogs with dry coat problems.

It is not true that bringing an outdoor dog inside for a few hours will make it more susceptible to the cold outdoors. Dogs are extremely adaptable, provided they have adequate shelter and a good coat. Putting an indoor dog outside for long periods in the winter is not a good idea, especially if it hasn't a good winter coat or is a chronic shedder.

With patience, you can habituate your dog to a vacuum cleaner, and a daily rubdown with the vacuum nozzle is an easy way of coping with a chronic shedder. Most important of all, try to keep dogs away from direct sources of heat, since when they "toast" themselves, they are more likely to become chronic shedders.

A common query is how to get rid of recurrent flea and worm infestations. Of the worm parasites, tapeworms are often linked with fleas. The tapeworm spends part of its life cycle in the flea and the flea then infests the dog. With this kind of tapeworm, it is essential to get rid of fleas, otherwise the dog will be reinfested after it has been wormed.

Children will not get pinworms from puppies. They get them from infested playmates at school. Puppies are often born with roundworms and hookworms and should, therefore, be checked by your vet and dewormed. *Never* buy worm medicine over the counter. Worm your dog only on the advice of your veterinarian using only drugs he prescribes. Never give worm medicine just because your dog gets thin or goes off its food. Such home doctoring more often makes the dog sicker than ever. Recurrent hookworm infections in your dog probably come from keeping the dog in the backyard or in a pen on the ground. It is in the earth that the worms develop. When they mature, they reinfest your dog. The best preventive here is to provide your dog with a concrete surface, wooden slats to rest on or gravel that will drain well.

Fleas (and ticks), except in warmer Southern states, have a season, proliferating in mid to late summer. Dogs often chew or lick and scratch just one part of their bodies when they are badly infested with fleas. This leads to the development of a moist, raw "hot spot." People waste time treating the spot while they should be getting rid of the fleas. Some dogs will also develop acute allergies to fleas.

The best treatment is a regular dip or sponge-down with a medicated shampoo approved by your veterinarian. Powdering every other day between dips also helps. In my opinion, flea collars protect only a small part of the body in a large dog and some pets do become sick when they wear them. A flea powder medallion under the neck is safer and just as effective.

Since the fleas will develop in your house, it is imperative to vacuum all carpets, drapes, armchairs, sofas and cracks and crevices in the floor. Then call in the exterminator. Often when the family comes home from summer vacation, they are greeted by a host of hungry fleas that have hatched while they were gone. Don't forget to treat pet and house at the same time and to repeat treatments every ten to fourteen days, and from then on as needed, because some fleas will probably still be developing in remote corners of the house. Sprinkling a teaspoon or so of brewer's yeast into your dog's food is said to help keep fleas off the dog. This is also a good source of B vitamins and should be given to dogs, fleas or no fleas. Those who let their cats and dogs roam free are even more likely to have infestation problems. So another way to fight fleas is to confine your pet to make flea infestation less likely.

I am frequently asked what is the best way to help a dog settle down quickly and not miss its owners when it is left at a boarding kennel during vacation periods. Some dogs do become hysterical or depressed, refuse to eat and become so rundown that they can become ill. So how to make things less stressful? I have found that taking the dog to the kennel a week or so before you are due to leave, just for an overnight stay, helps a great deal. The dog has a chance to get used to the place and since he has been picked up once, he will be less likely to feel totally abandoned when you leave him there when you go on vacation. Take some of his toys, blanket and basket along and an old (unwashed) T-shirt or sweater that smells of you. Even very dependent dogs seem to adapt well once these steps are taken.

Why do dogs eat their vomit? This does seem rather distasteful, but it is not unnatural. A bitch will often regurgitate food for her pups. Adult dogs who vomit (and who are not sick) will do this when they have eaten too quickly. A second eating may help the digestive processes. As for eating feces, this extremely unpleasant behavior is not normal in dogs, with the exception of mother dogs cleaning up after their pups. I have heard of housebroken dogs having accidents in the house and quickly eating up their mess. This is very rare, yet understandable. Regular stool eating, coprophagia, is a vice or bad habit acquired in puppyhood or in dogs who are caged or penned and who are bored with nothing to do all day. The latter respond well if given regular exercise and toys to play with—a willow stick or length of garden hose to chew and shake around are ideal. The vice in puppies simply requires consistent discipline and keeping the pup on a leash when he is outdoors so he can be controlled in time. Some nutritionists theorize that some stool-eating dogs lack certain essential nutrients. Providing a little raw liver or brewer's yeast each day does sometimes seem to help. Some dogs like to steal droppings out of the cat's litter tray. The best solution here is to put up a gate or wedge the door so that only the cat has access to its toilet.

Rolling in filth is perhaps the next most obnoxious thing dogs do. My answer as to why they do it is based upon the knowledge that they have a highly developed sense of smell, so that "wearing" an odor on their bodies may be as pleasant for them as it is for us (a more "visual" species) to wear nice clothes. As some people like to dress in a "loud" or flamboyant style, so dogs enjoy smelling strong or "loud." Wolves like to roll in meat before they eat it: carrying a smell that the animal likes on its body may be very pleasant for it. Since this is a deeply ingrained instinct, it is hard to control. Don't let your dog roam free, and if he is a roller, a touch of cheap perfume or aftershave behind each ear now and then, before you take him for a walk, will help considerably.

Problems and questions arise with dogs outdoors, too. What do you do when you meet unfriendly dogs? If you don't have your dog with you, don't run. Stand quite still and say "hi" to it, trying to hide your fear. Don't stare at it. If it looks like it is going to attack you (remember, most dogs bark more than they ever bite), back off slowly to increase your distance, since you are probably on his territory.

Sometimes simply ignoring the dog and walking slowly away at an angle (don't turn right around and face away from him) will suffice.

When you meet an aggressive dog with your dog on its leash, play it cool. Don't try to get between the animals or pick yours up protectively—you may get bitten. Give your dog plenty of leash, talk in a quiet, friendly and reassuring voice and the chances are the two dogs will just growl, take turns standing still while the other sniffs, have a ritual leg-up piddle and part amiably. Owners who shout and scream at another dog incite theirs to be aggressive or defensive and usually start the dog fight themselves.

What do you do if your pooch likes to chase cars, cyclists, joggers or children? Chasing is instinctive behavior and a normal canine response. Simply keep him restrained in the yard. No dog should be allowed free if it can't be controlled.

Excessive barking is an all-too-common problem and one that raises neighbors' hackles, too. I do not endorse the use of antibark collars. Simple conditioning is most effective. Shout "Quiet Fido" and give the dog one squirt in the face with a plant mister spray. After a few trials, the dog should learn to be quiet on command and won't need a shot in the face anymore.

Persistent barkers when you are out of the house and house-wreckers who tear things up when you're gone make up a large percentage of the behavior problem queries I get. Most dogs don't like to be left alone for extended periods, such as when the owner goes off to work. So what do you do? Some dogs will be happy if a radio is left on, or when they are given several of their own toys to play with. Others respond well to having a companion—another dog or a cat in the house. Very often, though, the person should not have gotten a dog in the first place. It is unrealistic and unfair to expect an active, dependent dog to accept spending all day alone in a small apartment or in one room of the house. Cats adapt better to such a life-style than dogs and one or two cats can be more fun to come home to than a distressed dog who has been barking or wrecking the house all day.

Some dogs will even become unhousebroken. Being unhousebroken can be a sign that your dog is unhappy or frustrated about being left alone. But if your dog is drinking excessively or is aging, a lapse of indoor manners could have a clinical cause and your veterinarian should investigate. Old dogs with kidney problems, for example, tend to drink more and are more likely to have accidents in the house if they aren't taken out more often than younger dogs with normally functioning kidneys.

NEUTERING

Another group of most asked questions about dogs concerns *neutering.* The best age to neuter depends somewhat upon your veterinarian. It should not be done until your dog is just about full-grown and is most safely done when your dog is not in heat. The chances of hemorrhage and other complications are then minimized. Bitches that are neutered too young can have problems urinating later in life because the external genitals are too small. Spaying is the term given to neutering or sterilizing a female dog. Both ovaries and the uterus are removed. This is major surgery and is done under a general anesthetic. It will not have any adverse effects on your dog's psychology, nor will it make her fat afterward, provided her diet is carefully regulated and she gets plenty of exercise.

Neutering male dogs involves removing both testicles. Tying off the tubes (vas deferens) will make the dog sterile, but will not eliminate his sex drive. Neither will tubal ligation in the bitch. There's really little point in having a dog, male or female, tubally ligated. Castrating a male dog is often desirable, since it does often reduce aggressiveness toward other dogs and also lowers your dog's sex drive and eagerness to go out and roam in search of a mate. Neutering does not make a male dog turn soft or effeminate and he should still be a good watchdog. Advantages of neutering dogs, other than having an easier-to-manage pet, include a reduced incidence of prostate problems and elimination of possible tumors of the testicle in males, and minimization of the chances of breast cancer and elimination of the possibility of ovarian tumors and uterine diseases in female dogs.

HELPING DOGS OVERCOME "AUTO-PHOBIA"

Many dogs suffer from "auto-phobia," fear of riding in an automobile. Often this phobia is triggered by the dog's being taken by car to visit the veterinarian or dog groomer, or for a sojourn at a boarding kennel. If the experience is unpleasant, the next time the dog is put in the car it may panic, making the association that the car ride will end up with a painful or stressful episode. And the apprehension persists each time the dog goes for a car ride. Auto-phobia can also arise as a consequence of the owner's apprehension while driving, or if the dog experiences motion sickness.

Motion sickness can be alleviated by treating the dog with

Dramamine half an hour before the ride. Your veterinarian can prescribe the right dose, which varies with the dog's size and temperament.

Motion sickness can be aggravated by general apprehension (and vice versa), so one of the best cures for auto-phobia is desensitization. Begin by simply sitting in the car with the dog, rewarding it with praise and tidbits of food for being quiet and calm. Fifteen minutes should be spent with the dog in the car every day until it no longer pants or behaves in an agitated way. If there is no change in behavior after a week, ask your veterinarian for a prescription for Valium and medicate the dog half an hour before sitting in the car with it. Medication should be given every day for the first three days, then every other day over a period of six days.

Phase two is to switch on the car's engine so the dog gets used to the noise and vibration. Sound the horn once or twice during the fifteen-minute period in the car, and continue phase two for four or five days.

If the dog becomes agitated again, either return to phase one or help it cope with its anxiety with the Valium treatment regimen.

Phase three entails driving the car slowly for a few blocks, stopping and starting a few times over a fifteen-minute period every day for about a week. Don't forget to praise and reward the dog for good behavior.

With this kind of desensitization program—and you don't have to be too rigid about it—most dogs will soon overcome their phobia.

I don't advise you to drive with a nervous dog free in the car. It should be restrained in the back seat behind an adjustable wire-mesh screen, which most pet stores carry, confined to a crate or secured by a harness to one of the seat belt attachments. Many otherwise incurable dogs do well in a holding crate or pen, possibly because the crate helps them feel more secure.

No one should ever drive with their dog loose in the back of a pickup truck, even if it enjoys going for a ride. All such dogs should be tethered or crated, or they could jump or fall out, cause an accident or be injured or killed.

Index

aggression, 31–33, 152–53, 204–5
anal gland, 61
animal experimentation, xiii, 20–21
animal rights, *see* rights, animal
anthropomorphizing, 154–61
associative learning, 176
attack training, 126–27
attention span, 174–75
auto-phobia, 206–7
awareness, in animals, 3–17, 161–69

babies, and dogs, 129–35
barking, excessive, 102, 107
basic commands, 119
bathing, 145–48
beauty treatment, *see* grooming
biting, 127–33, *see* aggression
boarding, 203–4
body language, *see* communication
bonding, *see* socialization
"breath-talking," 53–54
breed, choice of, 156–58
    origin of, 20
breeding, 137

canine hysteria, xii
change, recognition of, 185
chasing behavior, 205
children, and dogs, 129–35
choke chain, 113–14
coat care, *see* grooming
"come" training, 118
communication, 28–37,
    vocal, 47–57
companionship, 102–6, 108
conscience, 16–17
controllers, 99
coprophagia, 204

death, awareness of, 69, 77–78
debarking, 52–53
detour test, 187
dexterity test, 187
diet, and coat care, 149
discipline, 156
    inappropriate, 120
discrimination learning, 191–94
disobedience, 153

displays, *see* communication
domestication, xi, 18–27, 39–40
    and intelligence, 172
    effects of, 89–92, 96, 99
dominance, 34–35
"down" training, 118
dynamism, 177

early handling, 84–86
earthquake, awareness of, 76
eating, excessive, 132
emotional attachment, *see* socialization
    disturbances, 7–8, 31
empathy, 10, 162
environment,
    deprivation, 93–96
    enrichment, 80–82, 84, 93–109
    right, 137
equilibration, 177
ESP (extra sensory perception), 73–74
exercise, 107
eye contact, 34

facial expressions, 37
feces, eating of, 204
feeding, 137
feral dog, 25
fighting dogs, 23
fleas, control of, 203

games, *see* IQ tests
God, awareness of, 77–78
"golden" age, 19–20
golden rules, 87
grinning, 37
grooming, 139–51
    social, 42, 106

habit fixation, 176
handling, early, 84–86
heart rate, and temperament, 82, 106, 182
"heel" training, 116–17
hidden food test, 184–85
hide and seek test, 184
history, of dog, 18–27
homing, 42, 75
"hot spots," 203
    skin problems, 149

house-wrecking, 205
howling, 40
Humane Society, xiii
humor, sense of, 10
hunting instinct, 205

imagination, 8–9
insight, 1–4, 8, 178, 197–99
insight test, 188
instinct, 1–3, 75, 98–99, 162
intelligence, 4–17, 172–178
internal inhibition, 177
IQ tests, 90, 171
    advanced tests, 190–99

jealousy, 132
jogging, 97–98

language, in animals, 47–57
learning ability, 172–178
    scale, 164
    see also IQ tests
learning sets, 178
loneliness, 107

manipulation, 168
    manipulative behavior, 7
marking behavior, 35–36, 40–41, 61–63
    urination marking, 35–36
massage, 140
"mechanomorphic," 166
memory, 174–75
    short-term test, 191
mimetic behavior, 7
mimic learning, 178
"minding," behavior, 10
misbehavior, 153
miscommunication, 158
mistreatment, 152–54
moral sense, 8, 16–17, 78
motion sickness, 206–7
mounting, 31

neophobia, 80, 90
neutering, 206
nutrition, and coat, 149

object consistency, 173
observational learning, 7, 178
obesity, 96
odor, fear of, 61
    test of, 296–97
olfactory sense, 59–65
origin, of dog, 18
outdoor living, 100–2
overdependence, 104
overindulgence, 126

panting, 37
parasites, 202–3
parenting, 80
pariah dog, 25
passive submission, 30–31
Pavlov's superdog, 177
people, fear of, 86
permissiveness, 99
petting, effects of, 140
pheromones, 59–60
place learning, 196
play-bow, 30
"play-face," 37
pleasure bond, 80
protective instinct, 126
PSI-trailing, 70–73
psychic abilities, 67–78
    behavior, 43
punishment, 153

purebred dog syndrome, 99
puzzle boxes, 198–99

reasoning, 1–6, 8, 178
    test of, 197–99
reinforcement, 173
retention, in learning, 174
right and left test, 186
rights, animal, 82, 136, 151, 161–69
roles, of dogs, 18–27
rolling behavior, 65, 204

scent tests, 196–97
search and find test, 197
search image, 174
self-awareness, 162
    sense of, 10–11
separation anxiety, 107
sex drive, 99
short-term memory, 196
shyness, see timidity
sibling rivalry, 132
"silver" age, 20
"sit" training, 118
skin care, see grooming
skin disorders, 201–2
    diseases, 149
smell, sense of, 59–65
social behavior, 40–41
    responsiveness, 180–83
    scraping, 40–41
sociability test, 187–88
socialization, 79–84, 86
souls, animal, 166
sounds, see communication
    vocal, 40
spaying, 206
"speciesist," 164–65
"stay" training, 118
stimulus, generalization, 176
superiority, human, 165–66
supernature, 67–78
symbolic behavior, 7

tail docking, 43–44
talking animals, 54–57
teeth, care of, 148–49
temperament, 82, 86, 156–58
    tests of, 180–84
thinking, ability, 1–17
time-event learning, 178
timidity, 82, 84, 86–87, 124
"tool" using, 190–91
training, 111–21, see also IQ tests
    watchdog, 123–128
trainability, 111–12
tricks, teaching, 4
"tube" test, 185–86

unhousebroken, 107, 205
urination marking, 35–36
    submissive, 31

vacation stress, 107
veterinary preventive medicine, 136
visual discrimination test, 191–92
vivisection, xiii, 20–21
vocal communication, 47–57
vocalizations, 40
vomeronasal organ, 60–61
vomiting, 204

watchdog, training, 123–28
wolf, 23–24
wolf-dog hybrids, 25
words, comprehension of, 12–16, 195–96
worming, 202–3

210